Monuments of Grace

Living a Life Laid Down in Authentic Worship

Wes Pickering

Copyright © 2018 Not Enough Words
All rights reserved.

ISBN: 978-0692116654

http://wespickering.com
http://notenoughwords.com

Cover art by Kevan O'Connor. Cover design by Wes Pickering.

Scripture quotations marked HCSB®, are taken from the Holman Christian Standard Bible®, Copyright © 1999, 2000, 2002, 2003, 2009 by Holman Bible Publishers. Used by permission. HCSB® is a federally registered trademark of Holman Bible Publishers. All emphases by the author.

Scripture quotations marked NLT are taken from the Holy Bible, New Living Translation, copyright ©1996, 2004, 2007, 2013, 2015 by Tyndale House Foundation. Used by permission of Tyndale House Publishers, Inc., Carol Stream, Illinois 60188. All rights reserved. All emphases by the author.

Scripture quotations marked NASB taken from the New American Standard Bible® (NASB), Copyright © 1960, 1962, 1963, 1968, 1971, 1972, 1973, 1975, 1977, 1995 by The Lockman Foundation. Used by permission. All emphases by the author.

DEDICATION

For my wife, Hannah. You continually point me to Jesus and model His unconditional love. Thank you for bringing so much joy in this journey we're on together. Thank you for modeling grace, compassion, and gentleness every day. I'm forever grateful to be running the race, worshiping Jesus, with you by my side!

CONTENTS

Acknowledgments i

Foreword by Joshua Silverberg ii

1 The Altar 1

2 Simply Yes 13

3 A New Name 27

4 A Grand Purpose 43

5 Because He's Worthy 53

6 Undivided 67

7 The Secret Place 83

8 In Thought 101

9 In Word 125

10 In Deed 141

11 The Wilderness 161

12 Make Disciples 190

ACKNOWLEDGEMENTS

To my spiritual fathers, with more gratitude than words can express: Pastor Ford Pickering, who is also my natural father, you are the single most profound spiritual influencer of my life, and I love you dearly! Pastor Steve Bufkin, who entrusted me with leadership at 15 years old—when it made no logical sense to do so—you shaped my understanding of the furious love of God. Bishop Dan Scott, who married me and my wife: more than anyone else, you taught me to love God's Word and treasure the beauty of Christian life. Pastor Henry Seeley, who adopted me and Hannah so quickly as family and shepherds us so well. I'm so honored to call you and Alex my pastors. I thank God for you all.

FOREWORD

I met Wes in 2017 at the altar during a prayer time at The Belonging Co church. As we prayed, I noticed how he seemed to shine with such a pure hunger for God. Little did I know, in less than a year, he would become an answer to prayer for me. Fast forward to present day: we have laughed and cried together. We've ministered together at classes, churches, on street corners, and in home groups and seen many people receive freedom and healing. Wes is the one person who I know I can call up at midnight to talk or pray with, and he'll be happy to take the call.

Monuments of Grace is a practical and inspired book that will show you how to pursue Jesus in a lifestyle of worship. It's so amazing to see church worship music trending lately. But if we leave church and, for just a moment, also leave our worship behind, within those four walls, we've missed the point. It's actually possible for our hearts to live in continuous affection for Jesus, for our souls dwell in gratitude, and to live daily from that constant worship place. This book will give you a way to practice daily the presence of God—more than a feeling, more the than anything you are up against—by learning to keep your eyes fixed on Jesus.

The Bible talks about how we are living epistles to be known and read by all people, and I can personally tell you that Wes is one of those people who leaves a trail of testimonies and love wherever he goes. He lives his daily life so that the Gospel is made known, and the people he meets encounter the true and living God. Wes is not only a compelling teacher, worship leader, and student of the Word, he actually lives it, has become it, and I absolutely can't wait to see all the good things God has planned for him as his future unfolds.

As you read on, expect to gain understanding and revelation of the majestic, all-consuming love of God. Learn who He says you are and how He sees you through His Son Jesus. I pray that the Holy Spirit floods your mind and soul with God's thoughts and that the simplicity of this love relationship and Gospel is made known to you in a more profound way then you could have imagined.

-Joshua Silverberg
songwriter, producer, artist

1 THE ALTAR

I can imagine the moment Jacob awakened. This was no ordinary dream! The rock, still hard beneath his head, drew him further back into consciousness, but his wonder only grew.

"This is no ordinary place!"

There was something more significant, more real, about the dream he had just woke from than any other in his entire life. Indeed, it almost seemed a slight to call it a dream, for it was as real as the ground he now lay on—even more so. Heaven had just come down and touched the earth where he lay.

His mind racing, Jacob collected himself, trying desperately to remember as many details as he could. No verbal description could capture the splendor of the angels he had seen going up and down the stairway that reached all the way to Heaven itself. The light had been intensely bright yet somehow more colorful than what he had ever seen before. The angels—strangely, he knew what they were even though he had never seen one before—each traveled with a sense of purpose, a mission they knew must be carried out. Not one of them appeared insecure in his purpose but traversed the stairway with simultaneous grace and power.

And there beside him was *He*, the One his father Isaac and his grandfather Abraham had spoken of! The words Yahweh spoke were immediately familiar; Jacob had heard his father and grandfather repeat them many times, but this time was different. This time the words were *for him*!

> "I am Yahweh, the God of your father Abraham and the God of Isaac. I will give you and your offspring the land that you are now sleeping on. Your offspring will be like the dust of the earth, and you will spread out toward the west, the east, the north, and the south. All the peoples on earth will be blessed through you and your offspring. Look, I am with you and will watch over you wherever you go. I will bring you back to this land, for I will not leave you until I have done what I have promised you."
> Genesis 28: 13-15 (HCSB)

Jacob responded to this extraordinary visitation from God by taking the stone that had served as his pillow the night before and setting it up as a marker. Then, he poured olive oil over it and named the place Bethel, which means "a holy place," and made vows to honor God with his life and to give the Lord a tenth of all his possessions.

For generations after Jacob, even after 400 years in Egyptian captivity, Israelites would pass by the stone altar and recall the story of their forefather and his Heavenly dream. Throughout the Old Testament, on many occasions when God revealed Himself in a powerful or unprecedented way, people would stop right then and there to build an altar, setting up stones just as Jacob did with the one he used as a pillow that night. **These altars served a dual purpose: first, as a place of worship to offer sacrifices before the Lord, and second, as a monument so that those who would pass by afterward might remember what God had done there.**

Often these places were given special names, sometimes a

renaming, if the place had previously been known by some other name. In the case of Bethel, the place had before been known as Luz, a royal Canaanite city, but by renaming it, Jacob took the first step toward standing on the promise Yahweh made in the dream to give him the land beneath his feet.

Seizing upon God's promise, Jacob acted immediately and staked his claim for the Lord's holy place, even though nothing about the region around him had yet changed. The old Canaanite kingdom was still there. Jacob didn't yet have any descendants to occupy the land. In fact, he was currently on the run from his older, stronger brother Esau, whom he had deceived and cheated out of his birthright and inheritance as the first born.

There was no logical reason why Jacob should even take the dream seriously, yet he received the words from the Lord in his heart and acted with the authority contained in them. That brief experience gave him a glimmer of hope which defied his circumstances. This was the Lord's land, not the Canaanites'. The God of his fathers was real and had chosen him to carry the great promises made to his forefathers.

Today, nobody remembers Luz. However, because of Jacob's altar, we still remember Bethel, the "holy place," and the dream he saw. There are now countless churches named after Bethel, even hospitals, colleges, cities, and record labels!

To sum the story up quite simply, God showed up, and Jacob responded. Jacob's reaction to that brief moment changed the course of his life, his descendants' lives, and the lives of countless millions of others throughout history.

Jacob was already a changed man, and the renaming of Bethel was a prophetic picture of what God was doing inside him. However, although his inward transformation would be just as profound as the outward transformation of Canaan, it's not as if Jacob's character were completely altered from that instant. He still had many lessons to learn and many personal flaws to overcome. In fact, his faith and integrity at that moment were just a seed of what they would be in the future, and his vows to God looked more like bargaining than what many of us would feel comfortable presenting to God today:

> "If God will be with me and watch over me on this journey, if He provides me with food to eat and clothing to wear, and if I return safely to my father's house, then the Lord will be my God. This stone that I have set up as a marker will be God's house, and I will give to You a tenth of all that You give me."
> Genesis 28:20-22 (HSCB)

But the journey toward realizing God's promises had already begun. It was irreversible. The culture of Heaven had been planted like a seed in his heart, and it had already begun to grow. Over the years, Jacob would learn to leave his pattern of conniving and manipulation behind. He would learn that trust in the Lord would deliver to him the wealth and authority he so longed for his entire life. Rather than viewing his brother as a threat to his livelihood, Jacob eventually learned that God had enough wealth to satisfy them both; and rather than fear or despise him, Jacob learned to honor and bless Esau, even as God had honored and blessed him.

For Jacob, it all started with a stone. The Bethel stone was a line of demarcation, both a beginning and an ending point, separating the old from the new. It was the moment he knew that God had marked him for the kind of greatness his parents had raised him to believe in, though it would not be the last time God marked his life.

Catching just a glimpse of Heaven and hearing God's words spoken over his destiny forever changed Jacob and altered the trajectory of his life. Whenever he faltered or wavered in his commitment, God would call him back to Bethel, back to the moment when he *knew that he knew*. For Jacob, Bethel was a place set apart, and for God, Jacob was a man set apart.

That idea of being set apart is something we will explore together in this book. It is a central theme at the heart of what we call worship. Jacob's story is an early picture of what

God intends to do through all of His children.

Christ set us apart and hand crafted each of us for the purpose of advancing the Kingdom of Heaven (Ephesians 2:10). Jesus perfectly articulated this calling when He taught His disciples to pray, "...Your Kingdom come, Your will be done on earth as it is in Heaven" (Matthew 6:10). Heaven is not just the place we go to when we die, it is what we have been commissioned by God to carry with us to the lost and broken people of the world. That is why when Jesus sent out His disciples on their first missionary journey in Luke 10, He told them to tell the people they ministered to, "The Kingdom of God has come near to you." Experiencing Heaven on earth always leads us back around to worship.

Worship is the culture of Heaven. It is what happens and will happen there day and night, night and day for all of eternity (Revelation 4). When we worship, we become cultural ambassadors of heaven here on earth. Worship was never supposed to be relegated to a few songs at church before the pastor preaches. It is the third strand that binds together our personal devotion to God and our outreach to the world around us. It is the catalyst that activates every aspect of a disciple's life.

Bishop Grange led my wife Hannah and I up the rocky terrain, winding through the Jamaican jungle to pray for an elderly church member. If there was a path he was following, I couldn't see it for the thick greenery as we did our best to make sure each step was on solid footing.

His church sits halfway up the mountain about an hour north of Montego Bay in a tiny community suffering from extreme poverty. Earlier, we followed a pothole-riddled road until it was finally too steep for our vehicles to go any further. Then we hiked the rest of the way to the tiny, one-room church building that sits in the center of a handful of even tinier houses. A spiderweb of dangerous-looking electrical wires hung low, connecting many of the homes to the single electric pole in the village next to the church. The biggest prayer request from his congregation that day was a new piece of corrugated tin to cover the gaping hole in the roof where the rain pours in during the wet season.

When we first arrived at the church, Bishop Grange, having never met me before, looked me up and down and asked, "What instrument do you play?" I said guitar, and he quickly disappeared somewhere into the jungle for several minutes, returning with a dusty electric guitar that could barely hold tune. He plugged it straight into the home-rigged PA system with a cone-shaped loudspeaker pointed outside to loudly broadcast the worship services to everybody on the mountainside. I played along as his daughter led the congregation in singing, and church ladies shook old wooden tambourines and plastic bottles full of rocks.

After the music, Bishop Grange prayed for members of the congregation who were sick and weren't able to come that day. As our missions team proceeded with skits and activities for the children, I asked him if he could take my wife Hannah and I to see some of sick church members so that we could pray for them. And so, we found ourselves following him through the thick Jamaican jungle, past lean-to huts and partially finished concrete homes with rebar sticking out where the owners had run out of money to finish construction (a common sight in Jamaica).

We arrived at the home of a blind woman in her eighties named Grace, and we met her grandson outside. He led us into an empty room where she lay curled asleep on a bare mattress.

"Granma, wake up," her grandson said. "There are missionaries here to pray with you!" Mama Grace stirred and told us in delighted whispers how happy she was that we had come to see her. She asked us to pray that she might regain enough strength to go to church again and regain her sight so that she might read the Bible again. We joyfully obliged, asking Jesus to heal this precious daughter of His. As we finished praying, Mama Grace, still lying in her bed, began to worship.

"My Jesus! I love you! I adore you! You are so good to me. Thank you for your love! You are so wonderful and lovely! My Jesus! My Jesus!" It was the most sincere and passionate worship I have ever heard. Tears poured down her face, and we joined in. As we lifted our voices, the atmosphere of that little room on the mountainside changed as God's presence flooded the space. It was as if light in the room got a little brighter and the air got lighter and sweeter. A sickbed became a sanctuary, and Mama Grace's praise opened the gateway to Heaven. Gradually, our praise grew quieter, and Mama Grace's voice returned to its whisper. "Thank you, my Jesus, for visiting me today." Then she turned her head towards us and smiled. "Thank you also for visiting me," she said before lying down again to sleep.

If you're holding this book right now, still reading, I will assume that there's something in you that desires a life of deeper worship or deeper purpose in God's kingdom. Perhaps you have already had an encounter with the Lord that has marked your life, and you've caught a glimpse of Greatness you know is worthy of a lifestyle of worship. Or perhaps, for you, there is a more subtle pull, something you can't quite put your finger on, drawing your heart to respond to God in an authentic way. You may have grown up going to church, or maybe this is all brand new to you. My prayer for you, wherever you find yourself, is that this book will draw you into deeper revelation about who God is and what His plan is for your life. My hope is that, like Jacob, you will respond to God in a way that changes the course of your life. Worship has certainly altered the course of mine.

Worship, in its full context, is much more than songs we sing at the beginning of a church service to get everybody ready to hear a sermon. A lot of times, what we call "worship" puts severe limits on the on the broader Scriptural context of what it really is.

When the band or music minister at church does a good job, we say things like, "That was good worship today!" Or when something about the church service stirs our soul, we might respond with sincerity in our singing; or we might lift our hands to God; we might kneel before Him in reverence; or perhaps we might even say aloud to the Lord, "I love you! I worship you!" and in our hearts, we really mean it.

There's nothing wrong with those moments. In fact, in some form or fashion, I believe they are necessary for a healthy Christian life. I hope you experience them often! As a worship leader, I'm thankful that my life overflows with times like that, but there is far more to worship than what we experience in a church service, even a very powerful one.

Perhaps it might be helpful to think of those experiences as concentrated, distilled moments in which the adoration of God is our primary activity. We certainly shouldn't neglect corporate gatherings or dedicated times of singing. The Bible very clearly prescribes these activities and exhorts us to sing, to lift our hands, and even to shout to God with loud voices! But there's more to worship than music or a church service. Indeed, the full Scriptural context of worship is deep and rich and should spill over into every aspect of life, regardless where we are or whose company we find ourselves in.

So, allow me to begin with a pretty basic question: what is worship, anyway? To find the answer, let's look at a passage from Psalms that Christ Church Nashville, which was my home church for over 11 years, recites together nearly every Sunday:

> Come, let us sing to the lord!
> Let us shout joyfully to the Rock of our salvation.
> Let us come to him with thanksgiving.
> Let us sing psalms of praise to him.
> For the lord is a great God,
> a great King above all gods.
> He holds in his hands the depths of the earth
> and the mightiest mountains.
> The sea belongs to him, for he made it.
> His hands formed the dry land, too.
> Come, let us worship and bow down.

> Let us kneel before the lord our maker,
> for he is our God.
> We are the people he watches over,
> the flock under his care.
> If only you would listen to his voice today!
> Psalm 95:1-8 (NLT)

In that Psalm, the author starts with an exhortation to worship, and then he tells us why: "For the Lord is a great God…" Worship starts with who God is, and the evidence for who He is is found in the things He has done.

Let me attempt to boil this down to its essence so that we can proceed with a functioning definition:

Worship is our response to who God is and what He has done through our thoughts, words, and deeds.

There's a lot crammed into that little sentence, and we'll take the time to unpack it as we go along.

We get a lot of our modern day church liturgy from elements found in the Old Testament, both from God's commandments regarding the Tabernacle and from King David's plans for the Temple in Jerusalem. The most obvious difference, however, between our worship services and the ones back then is our lack of animal sacrifice. We can be very thankful for that…church would be a lot weirder…and bloodier!

In the New Testament, God used the sacrifice of Jesus to forever break down the barriers between His presence and the people of the world. Through the death of Jesus on the cross, we get to enter into God's presence without guilt or fear or condemnation. His blood paid the price for everything, all our sin, all our rebellion, and even every time we fall the tiniest bit short of perfection.

The heavy curtain in the old Temple that once separated the common person from God's presence was literally torn from top to bottom at the moment of Jesus' death. No longer do we need a priest to act as a mediator between us and God because Jesus is the ultimate mediator. No longer do we need the slaughter of an animal to absolve us from sin because Jesus was the ultimate sacrifice. And death itself is no longer something we need to fear because Jesus conquered that too!

So, now what? Instead of fearing death, we get to live the kind of lives that God always intended for us. Let's look at something the Apostle Paul wrote in the New Testament:

> Therefore, brothers, by the mercies of God, I urge you to present your bodies as a living sacrifice, holy and pleasing to God; this is your spiritual worship.
> Romans 12:1 (HSCB)

Jesus' death and resurrection flipped the old way of doing things on its head! Instead of offering up an animal or some grain or wine as a sacrifice (things God, Creator of everything, doesn't need anyway), Paul said we should give our entire lives in sacrifice, and that's what worship truly is. We're giving everything we have, our bodies, our emotions, our dreams, and our desires to live for the glory of the Father. However, we don't do this in order to earn forgiveness or even intimacy with God. Although our mistakes and character flaws completely disqualify us from earning even a moment in God's perfect presence, Jesus' life was more than valuable enough to pay the price for everyone! We don't need to earn our way in; Jesus already did that for us. Now that we are covered by His grace, purchased at the ultimate price, we respond with worship!

We worship Him for who He is, and we know who He is because of what He has done!

In Christ, we are restored to our original, created purpose of bringing God glory. We are to make our entire lives like the altar that Jacob set up: a sanctuary of praise to God and a marker pointing others to Jesus through the way we love and the way we serve. This is the kind of life that should make the world around us stop and take notice, like the Israelites when passing by Bethel, that something significant has taken place.

The line of demarcation in our lives should be bright and clear. The old is supposed to be distinctively different from the new because we are now living monuments of God's grace.

Throughout this book, we will explore what it means to experience life as an altar of worship before God, for I believe this is what God has in mind for every Christian. As we study together, keep this Scripture in mind:

> If you make a stone altar for Me, you must not build it out of cut stones. If you use your chisel on it, you will defile it.
> Exodus 20:25 (HCSB)

This is God's instruction given to Moses immediately after inscribing the 10 Commandments onto the stone tablets. Although the original context refers to the literal stone altars of the day, there's an important principle here that should be applied to our worship today: God is not interested in worship that we can chisel out ourselves. He places no value on cookie-cutter forms and makes it clear that forcing every stone to look the same as the next is a defilement of His intention. In contrast, take a look at how God instructed Joshua to build an altar after Israel crossed the Jordan river into the Promised Land:

> After the entire nation had finished crossing the Jordan, the Lord spoke to Joshua: "Choose 12 men from the people, one man for each tribe, and command them: Take 12 stones from this place in the middle of the Jordan where the feet of the priests are standing, carry them with you, and set them down at the place where you spend the night."
>
> So Joshua summoned the 12 men he had selected from the Israelites, one man for each tribe, and said to them, "Go across to the ark of the Lord your God in the middle of the Jordan. Each of you lift a stone onto his shoulder, one for each so that this

> will be a sign among you. In the future, when your children ask you, 'What do these stones mean to you?' you should tell them, 'The waters of the Jordan were cut off in front of the ark of the Lord's covenant. When it crossed the Jordan, the Jordan's waters were cut off.' Therefore these stones will always be a memorial for the Israelites."
>
> Joshua 4:1-7 (HCSB)

Throughout the Bible, water is used as a symbol of the Holy Spirit. In Psalm 46 and Revelation 22, we read about the river flowing from the very throne of God. Rather than chisel our lives into identical cut stones, our goal should be to allow the Holy Spirit to rush over us like a river, for as long as it takes, until we are formed into the shape that God intends for us. Each of us will look a little different from the stone next to us. Sometimes, we won't fit perfectly snug next to each other, but God is not insecure about this. Worship that comes from what we can shape with our own hands has never been what God is after. Instead, we are called to co-labor with the Holy Spirit as we are molded into the shape He designs (1 Corinthians 3:9). God does the shaping, and we simply put what He created on display.

Allowing God to shape our lives involves an amount of surrender that many people aren't comfortable with. Sometimes, we wish for the Holy Spirit to be a quiet stream, peacefully washing over us, when what we really need is a raging river. Other times we'll long for the adventure of white-water rapids when God, knowing His divine purposes for us, produces only a gentle brook. But rest assured: God's wisdom will always transform us into far more than we could ever create by hammering away at ourselves.

As you read, I encourage you to set down your hammer and chisel. Instead, step into the river of God and allow Him to wash over you, shaping you in His kindness and power. He has already started an incredible work in your life, and He will be faithful to complete it.

2 SIMPLY YES

It was the end of July, a few years after college, and I was serving as the worship leader for a week of middle-school summer camp in North Carolina that I had been a part of for many years. Most years, I would spend my time between sessions having just as much fun as the middle school campers, joining them for games, swim time, and various forms of harmless mischief. That year, however, I was recovering from some sort of flu bug, and I spent the majority of my time between sessions alone in my cabin, trying to save enough of my voice and energy to sing the next set of worship songs.

To pass the time, I reread the four Gospels and the book of Acts. One of the most remarkable things about the Bible is that no matter how many times you read it, there's always something new that jumps out at you, and my reading that week was no exception. The passage that God highlighted as I read ended up being a defining moment in my life, and it seemed to come out of left field, from one of the most unlikely places.

In the middle of Matthew's Gospel (and again later in Luke), there is an account of John the Baptist, who baptized Jesus and prophesied that He was the Messiah. However, after this pivotal moment in history, John found himself in prison, unsure if the things he believed about Jesus were actually true. So, John sent his disciples to inquire of Jesus on his behalf, "Are you the Messiah we've been expecting, or should we keep looking for someone else?"

Jesus' reply is remarkable. Instead of an immediate verbal affirmation, He redirected John's disciples to observe what was taking place:

> Jesus replied to them, "Go and report to John what you hear and see: the blind see, the lame walk, those with skin diseases are healed, the deaf hear, the dead are raised, and the poor are told the good news. And if anyone is not offended because of Me, he is blessed."
> Matthew 11:4-6 (HCSB)

Jesus diverts John's attention away from his dire circumstances and instead teaches him to focus on the amazing things He was doing. *Who He is…as evidenced by what He has done.* It's powerful stuff, but that's still not the part that jarred me to attention.

> As these men went away, Jesus began to speak to the crowds about John: "What did you go out into the wilderness to see? A reed swaying in the wind? What then did you go out to see? A man dressed in soft clothes? Look, those who wear soft clothes are in kings' palaces. But what did you go out to see? A prophet? Yes, I tell you, and far more than a prophet.
>
> This is the one it is written about:
> "Look, I am sending My messenger ahead of You; he will prepare Your way before You."
>
> "I assure you: Among those born of women no one greater than John the Baptist has appeared, but the least in the kingdom of Heaven is greater than he."

Matthew 11:7-11 (HCSB)

Did you get it? Those last two sentences reached out of the thin paper pages of my Bible and punched me right in the face!

"Among those born of women no one greater than John the Baptist has appeared..." Jesus just said that John the Baptist was, up to that point, the greatest guy ever born! I was stunned! What kind of statement is that?

It rattled me. I don't know if you remember much about John the Baptist, but he was a wild man! A spectacle! He was filled with the Holy Spirit while he was still in his mother's womb. When John's Aunt Mary, pregnant with Jesus, walked in the room, the baby John leapt for joy inside of his mother's womb. From his infancy, John was set apart, living differently than his peers.

The Jewish religious system had a family order to who could serve as a priest in the temple, and John was born into that family, the Levites. However, the Jewish legal system also allowed for individuals to voluntarily set themselves apart for service to God by partaking in a strict set of vows, ordering their conduct for either a set period of time or their entire lives. These men and women were the Nazirites, and John was one of them too—a lifer! So John the Baptist was born into God's service, but he also voluntarily gave himself fully to it.

The Nazirites were a radical bunch. If you weren't a part of the Levite family, the Nazirite vow was the only pathway to Godly public service. Old Testament heroes like Sampson, Deborah, Samuel, Elijah, Elisha, and even New Testament Apostles like Paul and James were likely among the Nazirite ranks at some point during their lives. Their lifestyle was rigid, never eating or drinking anything made from grapes, alcohol, or vinegar. By law, they were required to shave their heads at the beginning of their vows and never cut it again until their consecrated time was complete. They were never to go near a dead body, even if it was a close family member. Any failure on this point, and they would have to shave their heads again and start over; the previous days or years of service counted for nothing. At the end of their designated time of service, the Nazirites would shave their heads once again and offer their hair on the altar's fire, along with an animal sacrifice.

Jesus counted John the Baptist as the greatest Old Testament prophet, even though John didn't experience any of the miracles that Samuel or Elijah or Elisha did. John's version of the Nazirite lifestyle was extreme! He lived away from other people in the wilderness and ate a diet of locusts and honey. It's no wonder that, in a pre-YouTube age, he could draw a crowd!

"Let's go see the crazy hairy man out in the desert who eats bugs and wears camel skin and dunks people in the river!" John the Baptist was not...how shall I say it? ...cool.

By contrast, I live in a cool city, full of hipsters who obsess over their beards and their organic, non-pasteurized cheese; obscure indie bands and raw selvedge denim jackets. I work in the music industry, and yes, even the *Christian* music industry cares about how cool you are...how good you look...how skinny your jeans are! My job is largely dependent on whether or not people like me. That sounds cynical, but to some degree, it's true. If people don't like me, I don't get hired. If I don't do a good job, I don't get asked back.

Do you know who didn't care whether or not people liked him? John the Baptist, and it got him killed! John made the wrong people angry at him by preaching against the governor's sin, and he wouldn't back down. As a result, he rotted in prison and eventually wound up getting his head chopped off. This is the guy that Jesus singled out as the greatest guy ever born, the greatest out of all the Old Testament prophets!

Clearly, Jesus' priorities and my priorities were very different. Add to it the fact that Jesus also said that those of us who live in this Kingdom, on this side of the cross, will be even greater than John. Somehow, even though I couldn't understand why, I knew that my life wasn't measuring up to the standard Jesus highlighted in John's.

I pondered that verse for the rest of the week, and on the 7-hour drive home to Nashville I prayed, "God, I don't really know what you want for my life. I don't know what it was that made you like John the Baptist so much, and I feel bad that I don't know why. Whatever it is that you want from me, I want to do it. Whoever it is I'm supposed to be, I want to be that. Please show me how."

I drove home that Sunday in silence. When I got home, I was exhausted but couldn't sleep. Somewhere around 5 AM, the next day, I knew it was pointless to stay in bed, and so I dressed and got back in my car. A close friend worked as a barista at a coffee shop across town and was generous enough to give me free coffee when I came in. I arrived as he was opening and spent much of the morning chatting with him by the the counter in between customers. He kept serving me samples of dirty chai lattes he was trying to perfect. Not being able to sleep, a steady flow of espresso drinks was the next best thing!

At some point mid-morning, an elegant woman in her mid-fifties came in to buy some loose leaf tea. She asked me to reach a jar on a high shelf for her, and I obliged without thinking much of it.

"Thank you," she said. "My hands…they don't work very well any more. I have terrible carpal tunnel syndrome. You see, I've been a writer my entire adult life, and I've always written on a manual typewriter. Over the years, it's wreaked havoc on my wrists and arms!"

"I'm so sorry!" I responded. "I'm happy to help you."

"I've tried everything I can think of," she continued. "When typing on computer keyboards, my hands still hurt. I've even tried voice-recognition software to do my writing, but it just doesn't work well enough for me to really get anything done. I'm afraid I might just have to retire, not that I want to. It just hurts so much all the time!"

My heart ached for her, and somewhere in that moment, deep inside me, I knew that the Lord wanted me to pray for this woman. Not just any prayer—I felt the Holy Spirit leading me to pray for her physical healing. I balked! My faith wavered, and what followed was a rapid, seconds-long debate with God about what He was asking of me:

"God!" I argued, "I don't know if this is really You speaking to me. I don't know who this lady is or what she believes in. She might not even be a Christian, and even if she is, she might not believe in supernatural, physical healing! I don't even know what my barista friend believes—I wouldn't want to weird him out or his customers! This can't be right... not here. This is the wrong setting for something like that. I don't want to violate this woman's privacy. This has to be my imagination. You can't really be asking me to do this!"

What I really wanted to do was say something nice and churchy to comfort her: "Well, I'll be praying for you." And then I'd say goodbye and perhaps pray for her later. Later when I was more comfortable. Later when I was alone away from hipster coffee shop regulars. Later when I wouldn't be embarrassed. The funny thing about that little phrase that I've heard from Christians so many times is that nothing of the sort exists in Scripture. Peter didn't look at the crippled man at the temple gate and tell him, "Well, I feel so bad for you. I'll be praying for you." Paul didn't apologize to the parents of the boy who fell from the window, "I'm sorry your son died during my sermon. I'll be praying for you as you grieve."

Jesus didn't send his disciples out with instructions to let the sick know they were being prayed for. He didn't even tell them to pray for the sick! He told them, "Heal the sick." Period.

> Heal the sick, and tell them, "The Kingdom of God is near you now."
> Luke 10:9 (NLT)

Nothing in me felt qualified to take on a commandment

like that. No part of me had enough faith to believe if I took that kind of risk, God would follow through and do what only He could do. In that moment, I was consumed by my own insecurity and inadequacy.

Just then, my cell phone rang, and I seized the opportunity to get away from my situation. I excused myself and chatted with a friend as the woman paid for her tea and left the coffee shop. I watched as she got in her car and drove away, and an overwhelming sense of remorse crashed over me like a tidal wave.

I told my friend on the other end of the phone call, "Hey, I'm sorry, but I have to let you go. I just disobeyed God, and I need to repent." I didn't explain. I just hung up the phone, feeling like total garbage. Thanking my barista friend for the coffee, I made my way to my car to drive home.

On the drive home, I fell apart. My body began to shake in deep heaves, and I wept bitterly. I was angry with God for putting me in that situation.

"What kind of crazy person are you trying to turn me into? How am I supposed to do something like that? What if nothing happens? What if I had prayed for that woman's healing and she walked away still in pain? How is that supposed to make me look? Better yet, how is that supposed to make *You* look? Wouldn't that damage Your reputation? Wouldn't that give You a bad name?"

Suddenly, God spoke loudly and clearly, and it stopped me in my tracks. It wasn't an audible voice, but it was intense and erupted both from within me and from all around me:

"I don't need a new PR person. I just need someone who will obey."

His words broke into me like a wrecking ball, and I cried out loud, "Father, I'm so sorry! I'm so sorry for disobeying you. I knew what you asked of me, but I didn't do it. Please forgive me! Please give me another chance. I don't care what it is. I don't care what you ask of me. I don't care who I'm with or what I'm doing. I don't care if it makes me look like a crazy person. If I ever hear your voice like that again, I'm going to obey. No matter what it costs me, I will give everything in me to do what you ask me. Please give me another opportunity!"

That prayer turned the next two weeks of my life completely upside down! Everywhere I went, people told me that they were sick or injured, and every time somebody did, I stopped and prayed for them. And I mean everywhere!

When the girl behind the counter at McDonalds told me she woke up not feeling so well that morning, I said, "Hey, I'm a Christian, and I believe that Jesus already payed for you to get well when He was beaten and died for you. Is it alright if I pray for you?"

"Sure," She said, looking a bit surprised. I reached across the counter and took her hands and said a quick prayer. "Thanks!" she said. "That's really nice of you!"

The man who changed the oil in my car, elderly ladies in the grocery store, customer service people on the phone, close friends, and complete strangers—everywhere I turned, somebody needed prayer for healing. I prayed for the waitress on roller skates at the Sonic Drive In. I prayed for the guy at the coffee shop who said he was an atheist but responded to my offer to pray, "Yeah, sure. That sounds good." I prayed for the waiter at the Mexican restaurant. At some point, I quit asking people how they were doing because I was tired of people who were handling my food telling me they were sick! But they told me anyway. I stopped whatever I was doing and prayed for them all.

The strange thing was that I had no idea if any of them received their healing because, at that time, I didn't know that I should stick around and check to see if anything had improved, but I decided to let God handle the part that only He could handle. So, I simply said "yes" each time God put somebody in my path. No one refused. Everyone said "yes" to receive prayer. Afterward, each person told me "thank you" or that they were really encouraged.

After two weeks solid of this, I was exhausted! It was after midnight when I realized that my dog was out of food. So, I drove to the nearby grocery store; and pulling into the parking lot, I prayed, "God, I'm tired, and it's really late. My plan is to go in, get dog food, and go home. But if there's anybody who I'm supposed to pray for, would You just make it obvious?"

As soon as I got out of my car and shut the door, a woman began yelling to me from across the parking lot, "Young man! Young man! Come over here!"

I sighed and walked over. She was an employee of the grocery store, an elderly African American woman. She told me, "Young man, you look like you've got some kind of… energy or something! I don't know what that is, but I need me some of that!"

I shook my head, "Ma'am, to be honest with you, I'm exhausted! If you see anything in me right now, it must just be Jesus!"

Her eyes lit up, "Ooh! I *love* Him!"

I laughed out loud! "Me too! Let me pray for you!" I took her hands and prayed for God to fill her up with strength and energy and joy.

"Wow, baby! I feel good! Really good! I'm here working the graveyard shift at the deli counter, and I'm gonna have a good night tonight! Thank you! Thank you so much, sweetie!"

And just like that, things returned to normal again… mostly. After those two weeks, I didn't have sick people coming up to me everywhere I went any more, but I had learned a life-changing lesson. Never again will I consciously walk away from something I know God is asking of me. Whatever the situation may be, my prayer remains the same: "God, the answer is 'yes' in advance—just don't let me miss it!"

That experience helped me to understand that worship is about far more than the songs we sing: it's about the actions and heart motivations that back our words up. In Matthew 15, Jesus' sobering rebuke of the Pharisees was, "'These people honor me with their lips, but their heart is far from me." Let that never be said of me!

I am incredibly grateful for the second chance God gave me to be obedient and for His faithfulness to test me in my commitment. Those weeks shook off a lot of old fears I had about sharing my faith with others and practical ministry to the people around me.

To this day, I still stop and pray for sick people frequently, and there is no more fear in me. Instead, I now feel the Father's pleasure! Along the way, I have collected some amazing testimonies of God's healing power.

You see, like John the Baptist, anyone who is born again in Jesus has been born into the priestly family. Whether you grew up going to church or Christianity is completely new to you, it doesn't matter. You have been grafted into the Levites, God's tribe of priests!

> You are a chosen race, a royal priesthood,
> a holy nation, a people for His possession,
> so that you may proclaim the praises
> of the One who called you out of darkness
> into His marvelous light.
> - 1 Peter 2:9-10 (HCSB)

You were born for this!

But there's another layer. Also like John the Baptist, we have the opportunity to voluntarily give our lives up for God's service. This is not about your occupation. It makes no difference whether you're a pastor, a fishing boat captain, a school teacher, a lawyer, a TV presenter, or a shoe salesman. You can live your whole life as an offering of worship to God, with everything laid down in surrender, "a living sacrifice." God is calling us all into it! Like Paul, I exhort you to live your life with nothing held back, a consecrated sacrifice to God, just as Jesus made himself a consecrated sacrifice on our behalf.

We can learn a lot about what it means to live a consecrated life by studying the Old Testament example of the Nazirites. Theirs was a life of voluntary dedication. They consecrated both what was inside (the food and drink that they would partake, a representation of God's Word) as well as what was outside (their hair, a representation of the glory of God upon their lives). Some of the most crucial moments in Israel's history pivoted on the actions of these radical men and women because they chose to live set apart for God's mission, even during seasons when the rest of the nation lived in open rebellion against Him.

There is a key difference, however, between our role as consecrated servants and the Nazirites under the Old Covenant. In the vows that God dictated to Moses, the Nazirites' success or failure hinged on how perfectly they were able to execute the requirements for service. Especially with regards to being defiled by a dead body, if the Nazirite failed to uphold his or her vows, they had to start all over again.

> "If someone suddenly dies near him, defiling his consecrated head of hair, he must shave his head on the day of his purification; he is to shave it on the seventh day. On the eighth day he is to bring two turtledoves or two young pigeons to the priest at the entrance to the tent of meeting. The priest is to offer one as a sin offering and the other as a burnt offering to make atonement on behalf of the Nazirite, since he sinned because of the corpse. On that day he must consecrate his head again. He is to rededicate his time of consecration to the Lord and to bring a year-old male lamb as a restitution offering. But do not count the previous period, because his consecrated hair became defiled.
> -Numbers 6:9-12 (HCSB)

Even if it was an accident, being anywhere near a dead body was counted against the Nazirite as sin, and the glory of God could no longer rest on them. They they would have to shave their heads and start over.

In the book of Judges, we see that Sampson compromised himself again and again, flirting with the edges of his vows. Finally, Sampson made then disastrous decision to tell his secret to the enemy, and once his hair was cut, the glory of God left him. This man who once took on entire army garrisons by himself was completely helpless. His failure to keep the vow cost him everything.

Thankfully, it is not so with us on this side of the cross. Because Jesus lived a sinless life, He once and for all paved the way for us to walk in His perfection. We are not bound by our failures but bound to His righteousness (Romans 10). We are not made unclean by coming into contact with what is contaminated but have the authority to bless the things that God has redeemed (Acts 10). We are not defiled by dead things but commissioned to bring life to what has died (Matthew 10)!

Our mission is now a joyous one, a victorious surrender! We start from the position of Jesus' total success, and no longer do we need to start from scratch when we make a mistake. Instead we go from strength to strength, from grace to grace, and from glory to glory! Because the Holy Spirit lives inside of us, we no longer begin from a position of earthly weakness but from Heavenly strength. This is why Jesus said that even "the least of these in the kingdom of Heaven is greater" than John the Baptist.

We have access to something that John did not—Jesus' victory over the cross and the grave! We now live in a season of history that John and all the Old Testament prophets before him only longed for! Not only them, but even the angels of Heaven:

> Concerning this salvation, the prophets who prophesied about the grace that would come to you

searched and carefully investigated. They inquired into what time or what circumstances the Spirit of Christ within them was indicating when He testified in advance to the messianic sufferings and the glories that would follow. It was revealed to them that they were not serving themselves but you. These things have now been announced to you through those who preached the gospel to you by the Holy Spirit sent from Heaven. Angels desire to look into these things.
1 Peter 1:10-12 (HCSB)

You were created to be a part of something big! Now, let's respond to this amazing grace by answering the high calling that God has set before us!

3 A NEW NAME

"Can anyone tell me what is the most frequently used word in the New Testament to describe the followers of Jesus?" My dear friend and long-time mentor Pastor Steve Bufkin smiled behind his mustache as hands went up around the room full of students.

"Christians?" asked one. "Believers?" asked another.

"No," said Bufkin. "Those are good ones, but they're not the *most common* word. Any other guesses?"

"Faithful?" "Children?" As more and more of the young people in the room took a stab at the question, I suddenly realized that I didn't know the answer myself. Bufkin waited patiently for them to exhaust their guesses.

Finally, a young girl raised her hand and waited to be called on. She scrunched her face, cringing, and asked in a tiny voice, "Sinner?"

Bufkin's eyes looked like they might start tearing up if he gave her answer too much time to sink in. He smiled and shook his head affectionately. "No, it's definitely not 'sinner.' You want to know what it is? It's the word 'saint.' 'Saint' is how the New Testament, God's Word, describes Christians more frequently than any other word. Maybe you didn't realize it, but if you believe and confess that Jesus is the Christ, the Son of the Living God, the Bible says you are not a sinner any more. You are a saint."

Hagios is the Greek word that gets translated "saint" in the New Testament. It's used 61 times throughout, while the closest competitor *pistos* ("believers, faithful") is used 53 times. *Christiana* ("little Christ"), the word from which we get "Christian," is only used three times in the Bible. I like all of those words because each of them speaks to our new, true identity in Christ.

Notice that none of those words speak of our mistakes, our sins, or our brokenness because those things no longer hold any place in our identity before God. Instead, we are now identified by Christ's nature, by faithfulness and righteousness. A saint is one who is identified by his or her holiness and virtue; and that, my friend, is how God identifies you!

Identity is important. God goes to great lengths throughout Scripture to tell us what He really thinks of us, and the way we identify ourselves should be completely wrapped around the way God identifies us. The things we say, the thoughts we think, and the actions we take are all rooted in the soil of our identity, and when God's identity aerates and fertilizes that ground, we grow into the kind of people who bear the fruit of His Spirit.

Think back to Jacob's vision of Heaven. After he awoke from that magnificent dream, he not only set up the stone altar but also gave the place where he had slept a new name, Bethel. Even though the rest of the world still identified the location as Luz, an enemy stronghold, Jacob's vision now came into alignment with God's, and he renamed the place "house of God" according to the promise God made him in the dream.

As Jacob's life continued from that experience, he still had much to learn about God's nature and plan for him. Unfortunately for him and his family, Jacob still tried to shortcut his way into God's promises through deception and manipulation, and these poor decisions ended up causing a lot of pain.

There's a danger depicted in Jacob's story that I think many of us can relate to. Sometimes, we catch a glimpse of God's plan for our lives, or we sense the Holy Spirit whisper something to our hearts about our life's purpose. Those are exciting moments! However, oftentimes, we can see a finish line somewhere off in the distance, but the pathway there is completely obscure. Big visions, even God-size visions, frequently die out when we begin the journey without a clue how to get to our destination. Human tendency is to do what Jacob did: try to force an outcome regardless of what process it takes to get there.

This life of worship involves constant surrender to God, even surrendering the gifts He lavishes on us and the dreams He places in our hearts. There's nothing wrong with being blessed or having big vision (those are Godly things!), but when blessings or plans begin to supplant our pursuit of God Himself, we will always run into frustration.

Jacob hit wall after wall. Each time he got burned by someone, it reinforced his skewed worldview and made him less trusting and trustworthy. Still, God blessed Jacob according to His promise and not according to Jacob's behavior. God protected Jacob, provided him with family, and lavished him with wealth.

All the while, Jacob continued identifying himself as someone whom others would try their best to take advantage of, and he exhibited this view of himself by sneaking around, manipulating his way into what he thought was owed him. Sadly, along with the many blessings God poured out, Jacob also reaped the bitter harvest of his own deception. As he cheated others, others would cheat him. As he manipulated others, others would manipulate him.

The name Jacob literally means "heel grabber" because that's how he came out of his mother's womb, clutching onto the heel of his older brother Esau. That moniker pretty well shaped the course of Jacob's early life as he scratched and clawed his way to the top. Jacob seemed to feel that the only way to get ahead was to pull somebody else down, and so he left a lot of hurting people in his wake.

But God was determined to bless Jacob, not because of his character, but simply because that's how good God is! When God sets his sights on you as a target of His love, He will go to unfathomable lengths to demonstrate it in your life.

At one of Jacob's lowest moments, he gathered his family and possessions and sneaked away from his Uncle Laban's estate under the cover of night, not even giving Laban the opportunity to say goodbye to his daughters and grandchildren. God had blessed Jacob so much, but Jacob still didn't understand why, and rather than lavish those blessings on others, he hoarded them, afraid of losing what was actually a free gift from Heaven.

So, in the middle of all that chaos, God summoned Jacob back to Bethel, back to the place where it all started:

> I am the God of Bethel, where you poured oil on the stone marker and made a solemn vow to Me. Get up, leave this land, and return to your native land.
> Genesis 28:31 (HCSB)

On the way back to Bethel, Jacob prepared to stand face to face with his brother Esau, whom he had cheated many years earlier. Assuming that Esau would want nothing more than to kill him and take his possessions away, Jacob devised a scheme to butter Esau up by giving him a large share of the wealth he had acquired. Still, Jacob feared that even with lavish gifts, his brother wouldn't forgive his treachery, and he cried out to God in desperation:

> Then Jacob said, "God of my father Abraham and God of my father Isaac, the Lord who said to me, 'Go

> back to your land and to your family, and I will cause you to prosper,' I am unworthy of all the kindness and faithfulness You have shown Your servant. Indeed, I crossed over this Jordan with my staff, and now I have become two camps. Please rescue me from the hand of my brother Esau, for I am afraid of him; otherwise, he may come and attack me, the mothers, and their children. You have said, 'I will cause you to prosper, and I will make your offspring like the sand of the sea, which cannot be counted.'"
>
> Genesis 32:9-12 (HCSB)

Fearing the worst, Jacob had nowhere else turn but to the promise God made to him twenty years prior. Intense moments of desperation like that tend to feel like the absolute low points of our lives, but let me reassure you: when you've got nowhere else to turn but to God's promises, that's when amazing things happen! As we stop trying to control the outcome of our lives but instead trust in God's will, standing on the Word He spoke over us, that is when we begin to experience real breakthrough! In the natural, it's terrifying. Nobody likes to feel like they are out of options, but I can just imagine God smiling in Heaven saying, "Ah! I've been waiting for this moment!"

Something incredible happened in the wake of Jacob's desperate prayer. God visited Jacob again, not in a dream but in the flesh.

> Jacob was left alone, and a man wrestled with him until daybreak. When the man saw that He could not defeat him, He struck Jacob's hip socket as they wrestled and dislocated his hip. Then He said to Jacob, "Let Me go, for it is daybreak."
>
> But Jacob said, "I will not let You go unless You bless me."
>
> "What is your name?" the man asked.
> "Jacob," he replied.

> "Your name will no longer be Jacob," He said. "It will be Israel because you have struggled with God and with men and have prevailed."
>
> Then Jacob asked Him, "Please tell me Your name."
> But He answered, "Why do you ask My name?"
> And He blessed him there.
>
> Jacob then named the place Peniel, "For I have seen God face to face," he said, "and I have been delivered."
> Genesis 32:24-30 (HCSB)

There's something kind of bizarre and wonderful about that story! Let's break it down together.

Like he had done so many times before in his life, Jacob's response to God was to fight. I can't help but laugh at the line that says, "He (God) could not defeat him (Jacob)," as if God had somehow met His match! No, what this verse actually indicates is that Jacob's skull was thick, and the old way of communicating with him wasn't going anywhere! It's as if God finally said, "This just isn't getting through to you! Let's try something else!"

So, God dislocated Jacob's hip and forced him to walk with a limp for the rest of his life. It's an obvious symbol that God wanted him to stop struggling for success and rest in the free gift of His provision. Crippled people didn't usually fare too well in ancient society, but God intended to show Jacob that not even a physical impairment could preclude him from His lavish blessings. For the rest of his life, whenever Jacob was tempted to handle a situation out of his own strength or cunning, all he had to do was take a few steps, and he'd be reminded that he no longer walked according to his own ability. That limp was a constant reminder that God was providing for him, not himself.

Just like Jacob gave a new name to Bethel, God gave a new name to him. He told him, "Stop identifying yourself as Jacob. Your new name is Israel!" Israel literally means one "who prevails with God[1]." God wanted Jacob to stop identifying himself as a person who gets ahead by latching onto other people and start walking in the truth that latching onto Him would bring all His promises into fruition. Your name is no longer struggle, it's victory!

God kept after Jacob, not letting him forget about his new name. Later, when Jacob faltered and wandered away from the Promised Land, God called him back to Bethel and told him to repeat the steps that he had taken earlier in his life:

> God said to Jacob, "Get up! Go to Bethel and settle there. Build an altar there to the God who appeared to you when you fled from your brother Esau."
> Genesis 35:1 (HCSB)

When Jacob arrived at Bethel for the third time, he received yet another visitation from God, and God reminded him of his new identity and of all the promises that were still in effect:

> God said to him:
> Your name is Jacob;
> you will no longer be named Jacob,
> but your name will be Israel.
> So He named him Israel. God also said to him:
> I am God Almighty.
> Be fruitful and multiply.
> A nation, indeed an assembly of nations,
> will come from you,
> and kings will descend from you.
> I will give to you the land
> that I gave to Abraham and Isaac.

---

[1] Hitchcock, Roswell D. "An Interpreting Dictionary of Scripture Proper Names". New York, N.Y., 1869. Public Domain

> And I will give the land
> to your future descendants.
> Genesis 35:9-12 (HCSB)

God's goodness and grace were profound in Jacob's life, pursuing him and blessing him no matter how many times Jacob misunderstood or got it wrong. God's love for Jacob was radical, reminding him of his name, his new identity, time and again. Jacob went on to father a nation called Israel after his new name, and they inherited all the promises that God had made to their forefathers.

The Bible is full of instances where God pronounced a new name over an individual. Saul, the Pharisee who imprisoned and murdered Christians in the early years of the Church, had a supernatural encounter with Jesus on the way to persecute more of God's saints in Damascus; and God changed his name to Paul, simultaneously giving him a new name and a new purpose in life (to be His Apostle to the Gentiles). Paul would go on to write the majority of the New Testament, and it was he who exhorted us to "live our lives as living sacrifices."

God dictated John the Baptist's name to his father Zachariah before he was even born. Relatives of Zachariah and his wife Elizabeth didn't want them to name their baby John because it wasn't a family name, but Zachariah insisted because God had commanded him to do so. The name John means "the grace and mercy of the Lord[2]," and John would grow up to be the prophet who announced the arrival of Jesus to the world—Jesus, the very embodiment of God's grace and mercy.

Perhaps the most profound story of a name change in the Bible is that of Jesus' disciple Simon, the brother of Andrew. Simon was busy in his career as a fisherman before Jesus showed up in his life. The Gospel of Luke tells us the

---

[2] Hitchcock, Roswell D. "An Interpreting Dictionary of Scripture Proper Names". New York, N.Y., 1869. Public Domain

incredible story of Jesus and Peter's meeting:

> When He had finished speaking, He said to Simon, "Push out into the deep water. Let down your nets for some fish." Simon said to Him, "Teacher, we have worked all night and we have caught nothing. But because You told me to, I will let the net down." When they had done this, they caught so many fish, their net started to break. They called to their friends working in the other boat to come and help them. They came and both boats were so full of fish they began to sink. When Simon Peter saw it, he got down at the feet of Jesus. He said, "Go away from me, Lord, because I am a sinful man." He and all those with him were surprised and wondered about the many fish. James and John, the sons of Zebedee, were surprised also. They were working together with Simon. Then Jesus said to Simon, "Do not be afraid. From now on you will fish for men." When they came to land with their boats, they left everything and followed Jesus.
> Luke 5:4-11 (HCSB)

Seeing how marvelous Jesus is, catching a mere glimpse of His awesome power, immediately made Simon feel inadequate and dirty, but Jesus didn't address Simon in his sinful state. Instead, Jesus spoke of his Heavenly destiny!

"Don't be afraid" is the most frequent commandment in all of Scripture. Don't be afraid of your sin; Jesus has something better than that in mind for you. Don't be afraid of your inadequacy; Jesus has more than enough grace for you. Don't be afraid of your enemies; Jesus commands the very forces of Heaven. Jesus' first recorded words to Simon were words of mercy and hope.

Simon uprooted his entire life and livelihood and began a new life as Jesus' disciple, and in those three years, he witnessed the most astonishing events in human history. He saw Jesus heal strangers and family members. He listened as

Jesus taught about God like no one ever had before. He ate food that Jesus miraculously multiplied out of the most meager portions. He journeyed out with the other disciples, commissioned by Jesus, and healed the sick with his own two hands! He actually stepped out of his boat and walked with Jesus on the Sea of Galilee!

Simon paid close attention to Jesus and staked his entire future on who he believed Jesus to be: the long-prophesied Messiah of Israel. To him, the evidence was overwhelming and still kept mounting. Jesus had to be the One that the ancient men of God wrote about! What other explanation could possibly suffice for all the amazing miracles and signs he was witnessing? As Simon recognized Jesus for who He really is, Jesus in turn pronounced over Simon who he really was as well:

> But you," He asked them, "who do you say that I am? "
> Simon Peter answered, "You are the Messiah, the Son of the living God! "
>
> And Jesus responded, "Simon son of Jonah, you are blessed because flesh and blood did not reveal this to you, but My Father in Heaven. And I also say to you that you are Peter, and on this rock I will build My church, and the forces of Hades will not overpower it. I will give you the keys of the kingdom of Heaven, and whatever you bind on earth is already bound in Heaven, and whatever you loose on earth is already loosed in Heaven."
> Matthew 16:15-19 (HCSB)

Jesus gave Simon a new identity and a new destiny, wrapped tightly around His own. The name Peter means "rock[3]," but for all intents and purposes, Simon wasn't exactly

---

[3] Hitchcock, Roswell D. "An Interpreting Dictionary of Scripture Proper Names". New York, N.Y., 1869. Public Domain

the best candidate to bear that designation. Simon Peter was impulsive, quick to speak without thinking or jump to inaccurate conclusions.

Nobody can knock Peter for a lack of enthusiasm. He boldly pronounced his undying devotion to Jesus, even scolding Jesus for talking about dying (Matthew 16:23). But Jesus rebuked him, knowing that Peter was looking at the situation with earthly eyes instead of Heavenly vision. Jesus didn't hold Peter's fervor against him, however. Even knowing the betrayal that was to come, Jesus' affection for Peter is evident in the prayer he prayed for him at the Passover Supper:

> "Simon, Simon, look out! Satan has asked to sift you like wheat. But I have prayed for you that your faith may not fail. And you, when you have turned back, strengthen your brothers."
> Luke 22:31-32 (HCSB)

Despite knowing that Peter would deny him, Jesus looked ahead to Peter's great, eternal purpose and prayed that it would come to fruition. Jesus prays for you too! Did you know that? Paul tells us in Romans 8 that Christ is seated at the Father's right hand, interceding for you. In your lowest moments, when you feel like you've lost it all, when you grow weary, Jesus' affection for you and His plans for your life ring in the Father's ears!

Finally, when soldiers came to arrest Jesus, it was Peter who whipped his sword out and cut off the ear of one of the arresting party. But Jesus, ever patient and loving toward His friend, simply demonstrated His own grace and power once more, placing the severed ear back on the man, completely healing him!

Later that evening, as Jesus stood on trial before the Sanhedrin (the council of religious leaders who wanted to crucify Jesus for blasphemy), Peter hit his ultimate rock bottom. Fearing for his own life, Peter denied even knowing his friend and Messiah Jesus. Jesus had prophesied that once

Peter denied Him three times, a rooster would crow, and hearing that awful sound sent Peter's world into a tail spin, and he ran out weeping, once again overwhelmed by his sin and inadequacy (Matthew 26:69-75).

After Jesus' resurrection, He went to visit His old friend again. Peter, ashamed of his denial of Jesus, had returned to his previous career as a fisherman, but Jesus pursued him with endless affection.

Jesus recreated the events of their first meeting, again miraculously filling Peter's fishing net so full of fish that he was unable to pull it into the boat. When John, who was fishing with Peter, realized that it was Jesus there on the land, Peter jumped from the boat and swam to shore as fast as his arms would carry him. Jesus was there on the beach waiting with a fire burning.

> "Come and have breakfast," Jesus told them. None of the disciples dared ask Him, "Who are You?" because they knew it was the Lord. Jesus came, took the bread, and gave it to them. He did the same with the fish.
>
> This was now the third time Jesus appeared to the disciples after He was raised from the dead. When they had eaten breakfast, Jesus asked Simon Peter, "Simon, son of John, do you love Me more than these?"
>
> "Yes, Lord," he said to Him, "You know that I love You."
> "Feed My lambs," He told him.
>
> A second time He asked him, "Simon, son of John, do you love Me? "
> "Yes, Lord," he said to Him, "You know that I love You."
> "Shepherd My sheep," He told him.

> He asked him the third time, "Simon, son of John, do you love Me? "
>
> Peter was grieved that He asked him the third time, "Do you love Me?" He said, "Lord, You know everything! You know that I love You."
>
> "Feed My sheep," Jesus said. "I assure you: When you were young, you would tie your belt and walk wherever you wanted. But when you grow old, you will stretch out your hands and someone else will tie you and carry you where you don't want to go." He said this to signify by what kind of death he would glorify God. After saying this, He told him, "Follow Me!"
> -John 21:12-19 (HCSB)

For every time Peter had denied Jesus, Jesus gave him an opportunity to proclaim his love and devotion again. In the beginning of this exchange, Jesus actually used Simon's old name, perhaps a stinging reminder of what he had lost. But Jesus' love fully restored Peter and reinstated his new calling as the patriarch of the Church. Despite his past denial, Jesus prophesied that Peter would not waver that way again, even to the point of death.

If you think about it, Peter's experience with Jesus uniquely qualified him to lead the Church. He learned to hold onto the identity that Jesus gave to him rather than the one he created for himself through his shortcomings. From that moment forward, Peter understood that it's not by our merits that we qualify for this new life of devotion, it's by Jesus' merits. God redeemed Peter's shortcomings and gave him the perspective he needed to extend that grace to others (namely the Gentiles, the non-Jewish people who virtually no-one believed were qualified to be God's people). The life of Peter is a comforting reminder that God isn't looking for the person who seems the most outwardly up for the task. He's looking for someone who, like Peter, will simply say "yes" and "I love you."

Satan would have liked nothing better than to paralyze Peter into believing that he wasn't good enough to represent Jesus to the world, but Jesus had other plans entirely. Just like with Jacob, when Peter was at rock bottom, Jesus met him back where it all started. He reminded Peter of his calling and purpose. How many times throughout the rest of Peter's life do you suppose he stood at the sea shore and reflected on those amazing moments with his friend the Messiah?

There are lots of parallels between Jacob's and Peter's stories. Both of them had radical encounters with God and vowed to spend the rest of their lives devoted to serving Him. Both received new names and new life missions to lead God's people. However, both wavered in their faith when the going got tough. Still, God pursued them with fierce devotion, demonstrating His limitless grace, and never allowed them to outrun their new names.

What is the name that God has given you? I encourage you to spend some time alone with God asking Him and listening for His answer. I can tell you this: it has nothing to do with your past mistakes and everything to do with His outrageous love for you.

Perhaps you feel like Jacob, like you're always a hair's breadth away from failure. Maybe you can relate to the wake of destruction and pain Jacob left behind him everywhere he went. Hear the Lord whisper to you that He is your success wherever you go! Listen to Him choose you as His ambassador of blessing to the world around You!

Maybe you feel like Simon, Simon the hot-head, Simon the unfaithful friend, Simon the sinner. Allow the Lord to set the breakfast table for you and restore you in His love. Perhaps what you need is to return to that place you first encountered Jesus and allow Him to remind you of your new identity in Him. He is kind enough to meet you there again.

The Bible has lots to say about your identity, especially in the light of Jesus' victory over sin at the cross. In Him, you are a friend of God. You are the Bride of Christ, the object of His affection. You are the light of the world! Every aspect of your life is made new in Him.

Peter, who went on to write some of the most beautiful texts in the New Testament had a few important things to say to you about who you are in Christ:

> Coming to Him, a living stone — rejected by men but chosen and valuable to God — you yourselves, as living stones, are being built into a spiritual house for a holy priesthood to offer spiritual sacrifices acceptable to God through Jesus Christ. For it is contained in Scripture:
> Look! I lay a stone in Zion,
> a chosen and honored cornerstone,
> and the one who believes in Him
> will never be put to shame!
> 1 Peter 2:4-6 (HCSB)

Here, it is evident that Peter finally embraced his identity as "the rock," because of his confidence in his amazing friend, The Rock! Peter extends that identity to you: you are also God's rock. You will never be disappointed by His faithfulness.

And there's that theme again: your life is meant to be the living stones built up into a place where God's presence rests. You don't have to worry about getting there in your own strength because God will always cover you in His perfect power. He will be faithful through your worst moments and continue to back up every promise He has ever made to you. You can be secure in your identity because it is backed up by His own. You are a "living stone" because your foundation is the Cornerstone.

4 A GRAND PURPOSE

Along with your God-given identity, as a believer in Jesus, you also inherit a grand purpose for your life. Actually, your Heavenly purpose long precedes the moment you accepted your new identity in Christ. It was envisioned by God before He even created the world (Ephesians 1).

The very first thing we read about ourselves in the Bible is astonishing!

> Then God said, "Let Us make man in Our image, according to Our likeness. They will rule the fish of the sea, the birds of the sky, the livestock, all the earth, and the creatures that crawl on the earth."
> So God created man in His own image;
> He created him in the image of God;
> He created them male and female.
> Genesis 1:26-27 (HCSB)

You were created to bear the very image of God! That alone makes you inherently valuable. I don't know if you already knew this, but you look a lot like your Father!

Satan does everything he can to obscure this truth. In the garden, he tempted Adam and Eve out of their out of their relationship with God. He did so by challenging their identity and God's goodness toward them. Filled with shame, Adam and Eve hid themselves away from God, covering themselves with whatever they could find. The image of God grew dim in their eyes, and all they could see was their failure.

But God, in his tenderness, addressed their sin and shame immediately by slaughtering a lamb (a prophetic picture of what Jesus would do for us on the cross) and making them clothing from the lamb skin. Adam and Eve disqualified themselves from their life in Eden, with nightly walks alongside God, but God immediately set to work redeeming humanity, restoring us into right relationship with Him. The consequences of sin are indeed grave, but the measure of Jesus' sacrifice is so much greater. There is no comparison between the two: Jesus is completely victorious.

There is a venomous theology that has seeped into the Church throughout history, namely that you were completely worthless before Jesus died on the cross and that even as a Christian, the only thing that's any good about you is Jesus inside of you. Like so many of Satan's lies, this one rings plausible in our ears because sin fills us with shame, just like Adam and Eve.

The language of shame often finds its way into our prayer and worship: "I'm just a lowly sinner." "I'm as worthless as pond scum, but Jesus loves me anyway (I've actually heard a preacher say this!)" Isaac Watts (whose hymns are still of incalculable value to the Church) actually penned the lyric "Would He devote that sacred head for such a worm as I?"[4] I love you, Isaac, but no! Jesus didn't come and die for worms. He came and died for his precious children who bear His holy image! Watts is borrowing this language from Psalm 22 (which we will discuss at length in Chapter 5) where David writes, "I am a worm and not a man, scorned by men and despised by people." However, it is vital to note that David's despair was rooted in how other men perceived him, not in how God saw him. Self-loathing statements like that might sound like

---

[4] Watts, Isaac. "Alas did my Savior Bleed? (At the Cross)". *Hymns and Spiritual Songs Book II.* Public Domain.

humility, but really they're the voice of shame and condemnation, a voice that devalues what God values.

The Apostle Paul tells us that in Christ, the old things have completely gone away and that everything we are now is made new in Jesus (2 Corinthians 5:17). Why then, would we go on clinging to an old identity as a "lowly sinner"? Certainly, over the course of our days, we still commit sin, but that is no longer where our identity is held. As we discussed in the last chapter, our identity is now as saints, co-heirs with Jesus. How could we ever expect to live a life of righteousness if we don't adopt our new identity as "the righteousness of God" (2 Corinthians 5:21).

Furthermore, how can we begin reaching the world around us with the love of Christ if we don't recognize others as being valuable to God? How can we offer love and value to others if we don't really believe how much God loves and values us?

Don't misunderstand me here—I get it. Sin wholly disqualifies us from relationship with God. In no way am I trying to cheapen the grace that Jesus extended to us on the cross. We didn't deserve it. Period. In fact, by our own actions, each of us fully deserves the brunt of God's wrath; and without the covering of Jesus' blood, we are completely exposed to that wrath. Sin creeps into every crevice of our being and corrupts completely, and no one is exempt. Without Jesus, we weren't just drowning in our transgressions, we were dead in spirit. Dead-dead. We didn't just need an IV or a defibrillator because, like Lazarus in the tomb, we were already decomposing. Stinky dead. Only the life-giving power of Jesus could save us because we were long gone!

However, understanding that Jesus gave Himself for us because we are valuable to Him is vital in our response to His grace, what we do with our lives, and how we treat the world around us. No nails could have ever held Jesus to the cross. No, it was love that held Him there until He breathed His last breath!

Paul tells us as much in his letter to the Romans:

> For while we were still helpless, at the appointed moment, Christ died for the ungodly. For rarely will someone die for a just person — though for a good person perhaps someone might even dare to die. But God proves His own love for us in that while we were still sinners, Christ died for us! Much more then, since we have now been declared righteous by His blood, we will be saved through Him from wrath. For if, while we were enemies, we were reconciled to God through the death of His Son, then how much more, having been reconciled, will we be saved by His life! And not only that, but we also rejoice in God through our Lord Jesus Christ. We have now received this reconciliation through Him.
> Romans 5:6-11 (HCSB)

Sin, while absolutely disqualifying you from relationship with God and exposing you to His wrath, does not preclude you from His love. Perhaps the most famous verse in the Bible, John 3:16, makes it abundantly clear: God sent His only Son to die for you *because* of how much He loves you! Anything Jesus loves is valuable, including sinners…including people who don't know Him or have rejected Him.

On several occasions, Jesus used different parables to describe His heart towards the world's lost people. In Matthew 18, Jesus describes us as "lost sheep," so valuable that He would leave 99 others to go find just one. In Luke 15, Jesus describes us as a valuable coin that is worth stopping everything to search for until found. He says when we are found again, the angels in Heaven rejoice! Also in Luke 15 is the famous parable of the Prodigal Son in which the lost person is portrayed as a son who, having squandered his entire inheritance, comes home to find his father running to greet him, throwing him a feast, clothing him with the best robe and a ring. In none of those parables does Jesus even hint that we're worthless worms. No! We're his precious children, the possession He values most!

One of my best friends, just today as I wrote this chapter, welcomed his first baby into the world, a beautiful, healthy son who already looks like a perfect mixture between his mom and dad. When he messaged me to tell me his son had arrived, he said, "I have shed a few tears. God is good. Holding my son is a life-changing thing."

I replied, "If you can, stop for a moment and ponder the thoughts that Abba has about you."

He messaged back, "I have. It makes me teary. It puts the sacrifice of Jesus in a whole new light." If we, with our finite capacity, can love our sons this much, how much more affection does the Father, who is infinite, feel when he looks into our faces? How much more amazing is it that he chose to sacrifice his only Son Jesus to rescue us?

Satan relentlessly attempts to soil the image of God in you through sin. He tries to keep you from fulfilling your purpose by covering you with shame, but Jesus washes that away with His blood, simply asking you to repent and believe in Him. His righteousness qualifies us, once again, to walk with God in the cool of the day, like Adam did; and His victory gives us the means to reject sin and live holy lives. In 1 Corinthians, Paul refers to Jesus as "the last Adam," because Jesus completely reconciled what Adam lost in the Garden. God put the first Adam to sleep, opened his side, and from the rib, God formed a wife. The Last Adam died on a cross; His side was split open; and from the blood and water that poured out, God birthed His Bride, the Church. Sin makes us wretched, but God has never been content to leave us that way.

Having been made new in Christ, you are now restored into your original created purpose, to bring glory and honor to God! Remember the "living stones" passage from 1 Peter? That's what this is all about. Your life is a temple, an altar, the very place where God's glory rests, and your heart is His throne!

Look what else Peter has to say about your purpose:

> But you are a chosen race, a royal priesthood,
> a holy nation, a people for His possession,
> so that you may proclaim the praises
> of the One who called you out of darkness
> into His marvelous light.
> Once you were not a people,
> but now you are God's people;
> you had not received mercy,
> but now you have received mercy.
> 1 Peter 2:9-10 (HCSB)

That phrase "royal priesthood" is pretty remarkable. As I mentioned in Chapter 1, the Levites used to be the only ones authorized for service in the Temple. But now, *you* are both the temple and a priest. God cannot be contained to a building or to one tribe of people. He is with all of us who are in Christ!

Another thing that's illuminating about that phrase is that kings in Israel were never allowed to be priests. Israel's first king, King Saul, actually cost himself the throne by trying to take on the role of priest and make sacrifices to God on his own (1 Samuel 13). From then on, God decreed that the lineage for kingship would go to David's tribe: the tribe Judah. The two roles could not legally intersect. No Levite could be a king, and no king could be a priest.

However, just as Jesus' death on the cross tore the temple veil that separated people from the presence of God, it also mended the tear that separated priest from king. Hebrews 7 states that Jesus was priest and king, not because of his ancestry but because of the "power of an indestructible life." In other words, Jesus both pre-dated and outlasts the laws about who can be a priest. His rule is eternal.

Jesus now extends that priestly role to you, his disciple. You are invited to "co-labor" with Christ as a priest and a king. As a member of Jesus' royal family, you are an heir to everything He earned by living a perfect and sinless life. As a priest, you take on the holy responsibility of ministering to

God himself. Under the Old Covenant, only a Levitical priest was allowed to burn incense before God, but under the New Covenant, Paul describes your entire life as the very aroma of Christ offered up to God:

> Thanks be to God, who always puts us on display in Christ and through us spreads the aroma of the knowledge of Him in every place. For to God we are the fragrance of Christ among those who are being saved and among those who are perishing.
> 2 Corinthians 2:14-15 (HCSB)

Your priestly calling is to spread the aroma of Christ to the world around you! To be sure, not everyone will enjoy the smell, but God will! To Him, there's nothing sweeter!

Not too long ago, I attended a fundraiser for a pregnancy resource center (a cause that's near and dear to my heart). This particular event happened to be right smack dab in the middle of an election year, and it seemed like most people in the United States, regardless of political persuasion, were stressed out about the direction of the country. At the beginning of the event, a Christian band got up and played several songs, closing their set with a patriotic song about how great it is to be an American. Looking around the room, I was astounded by the crowd's response!

It was like stepping into a charismatic church service! People stood to their feet, raising their hands. Some people cried openly. Some people wrapped their arms around each other and sang their hearts out. And when the song was done, the room literally shook with thunderous applause. The atmosphere was electric! People shouted and cheered and clapped like they had just witnessed greatness.

My stomach turned a little, not because I have any problem with fervent patriotism or getting emotional about how much one loves his country. No, I was disturbed because this was worship. You see, the saddest thing to me is that this was primarily a room full of Christians, and the band had previously sung song after song about Jesus' saving grace and His resurrection from the grave. Those songs only received polite applause. But America…America got worship.

If you think about it, everyone in the world worships something, but many people simply place something other than God on the throne of their hearts. For some, it's their country. For some, it's money. For some, it's fame or power or sex. For some, it's the need to be independent. For others, it's the need to be needed. There's always something resting on the throne of every person's heart.

Every culture, throughout every period of human history, has worshiped something or someone. Humanity has always erected altars and sacrificed to idols. Even in modern, Western culture, people make sacrifices to their idols. It's what we spend our time and our money on. It's what consumes our hearts, what we get the most excited about. It's the thing that shapes how we treat others.

Why is this? I would submit to you that it's because humans are hard-wired for worship. It's what we were created for. Everyone, every person who draws breath, was made to worship; and we all do it, whether we realize it or not.

The Christian life is largely about sacrificing all of the other things we are tempted to worship and placing them on the altar before God. It's not that we can't be patriots or have money or enjoy sex or get excited at football games; but those things cannot supplant God's position at the highest place of our devotion.

God actually wants us to enjoy the things He created in this life, even the things He asks us to sacrifice. Don't believe me? Consider this amazing facet about Levitical sacrifice that has largely been lost in our modern theology: When any family brought their sacrifice to God (a lamb, for example), the priest would prepare it and place it on the altar where it would roast in the fire. Then, the family would share the sacrifice with the priest and eat the meal there in the presence of God (See Deuteronomy 14). For most families, this was likely the best meal of the entire year! The sacrifice was meant to be enjoyed, not at the expense of neglecting relationship with God but *in relationship* with Him.

What would happen if we, as Christians, stopped allowing the things of this world to supplant God on our heart's throne and instead began offering them up to the Lord? Then, in His presence, we enjoy all the gifts He has given us, fully aware that He is worthy to keep it all for Himself but loving enough to share it with us! I submit to you that any meal, whether it's a meager lunch of bread and fish or the finest banquet feast ever assembled, would taste immeasurably better if enjoyed in the presence of God.

If you read the books of Exodus, Leviticus, and Numbers you'll find that the Tabernacle was full of consecrated items, crafted and set aside exclusively for service to God. Each item was painstakingly made and cared for because it represented the holiness of God who dwelled there. You were no less painstakingly created by your Father. He crafted you into something more valuable than gold or silver and has chosen you as the resting place for His presence.

I encourage you to take an inventory of your life. Look at each aspect of what's valuable to you and how you spend your time, and ask yourself, "Have I consecrated this to God?" Think about what it would look like if you took those things, dedicated them to His service, and then enjoyed them in His presence.

Under the Old Covenant, the Nazirites exemplified what it looks like to live a consecrated life before God. With Christ, that life of consecration takes on new meaning. It's not about austerity or giving up things to try to earn closeness with God. No, it's about bringing our lives into order with our created purpose: to reflect the image of God to the world around us.

There might be things in your life that are detracting from the fragrance of Christ burning as incense inside you. There might be things that have been neglected because you didn't see them as valuable before. Maybe you have a talent that you're not using because you never saw it as worth anything before, but what would happen if you began using that talent as worship before God? It doesn't have to be complicated. Let's say for example that you're a good cook, but for most of your life you've only used that gift to satisfy your basic needs and occasionally entertain others. What might it look like if you used that to serve the Lord? Maybe you prepare a meal for someone in need. Maybe you host a Bible study at your home and cook for your guests. Or maybe…here's a wild idea…you just cook for yourself, the same as before, except now you become aware of God's presence as you prepare your meal, and you feast on Him as you prep your food. That might sound completely crazy to you, but I promise you, when you begin consecrating even the smallest details of your life, you'll be amazed at the number of times you're suddenly aware of the fact that God is with you. He loves spending time with you!

This fellowship with God is the very reason He created you. It brings Him glory and delight! With His Spirit residing in us, He now calls us to carry His presence to the world around us, to bring reconciliation to those who are still outside relationship with Him. We have been called to join in the ministry that Jesus began here on earth: going after the lost sheep, searching diligently for the missing coin, and welcoming the prodigals home. There is no more noble or grand work than this!

5 BECAUSE HE'S WORTHY

I was dumbfounded, nearly unable to process what my friend Matt was telling me. We were in his car, on our way back to my house from dinner, discussing a recent event where I had led worship. I was telling him some of the ways I try my best to foster an environment where congregations can freely and passionately sing together.

"Well, I'm probably not a good person to talk to about this. I don't ever sing in church," he said blandly.

"What?" I wasn't sure if I understood what he was trying to say.

"No. It just doesn't do anything for me."

"What are you talking about? You don't sing…ever?"

"Nope, not at church. It's just not my thing. I don't really get anything out of it, so I don't do it. It's cool if other people want to do it, but that's just never been something that I enjoy."

"So, what do you do in church while everyone else is singing? Just stand there?"

"Pretty much."

As a worship leader, this was a jarring revelation to me, especially coming from a close friend. Matt was somebody who professed Jesus as his Lord and Savior, a well-versed student of the Bible, and a music-lover besides. I had attended numerous concerts with him and heard him sing along with and cheer his favorite bands. This information just didn't add up.

I thought about what Matt said for a long while. At first, it was one of those moments that struck me as problematic on a gut level, but I couldn't seem to find the words to articulate what I was feeling. Here's this thing that I have dedicated my life to (leading others in song), but one of my closest friends just point-blank declared that it means nothing to him.

Finally, I answered him, "I don't know how to tell you this, but it's not really about you." He stared at me, puzzled. "Worship isn't about whether or not you *feel* anything. It's not about 'getting something out of it.' It's not about goose bumps or warm tingly feelings. Honestly, it shouldn't matter if you ever receive anything from singing because it's just not about you. It's about Him."

By nature, I'm a feeler. I love all the warm tingly feelings we sometimes experience in worship. I love the moments at a church service where God's presence feels thick in the room, like you could reach out and physically touch Him. By default, my first response to sensing God's presence is simply to cry. At times, it's been embarrassing because once I get weepy, it becomes difficult to form words, let alone sing on key. But I love all that stuff anyway. Still, at the end of the day, that simply isn't what worship is about. It's not about us, it's about God.

We worship God because He deserves it. It's not about trying to get something but about giving everything. Remember our definition of worship from Chapter 1?

Worship is our response to who God is and what He has

done through our thoughts, words, and deeds.

God has already earned our worship, simply because of who He is, and we see the evidence of who He is in all the things He has done. He is Creator, Savior, Redeemer, Healer, Provider, Sustainer. He is our Foundation, our Joy. He is eternal. He is good. He is holy.

But wait! I can hear somebody out there questioning the premise: *Isn't worship about more than just singing and the music we do at church?* Of course it is! But that doesn't mean we neglect those things as a part of our worship. We must not abuse the verbiage "worship is a lifestyle" as an excuse to eliminate praise and worship as a primary activity. The Bible is full of exhortations for God's children to sing, clap, shout, lift our hands, and yes...even dance.

Let me put it this way: consider an Olympic figure skater. For them, skating is a way of life! That way of life consists of intense gym workouts, ballet classes, gymnastics training, media interviews, photoshoots, strict diet regimens, and weeks of travel around the world. However, if at some point he or she does not strap on a pair of skates and take to the ice, they cannot call themselves figure skaters. The broader lifestyle and the primary activity must go hand in hand, each strengthening the other and giving the other purpose.

God is worthy of your voice. He's worthy of your exclusive focus and your declarations of praise. Even Jesus, who perfectly exemplified a lifestyle of worship, sang hymns of praise to God with His disciples (Matthew 26, Mark 14). He's worthy of our songs even through seasons where it doesn't involve any noticeable benefit on our end.

When my wife and I first met, we lived nearly 500 miles apart, and for the first five months of our relationship, we didn't see each other. Instead, we sent thousands of messages and spent hours on the phone together. For five months we got to know each other and learned to communicate. We talked and talked and talked about anything and everything. Finally, I drove from Nashville to her small town in Arkansas for our first date. As we sat across from each other at the little Thai restaurant near her home, neither of us knew what to say. We had already said pretty much everything over the phone or in messages, but that didn't matter. I wasn't asking her to say anything or do anything. I was simply happy to *just be* with her. And I told her so: "I'm so happy to be here with you!" She agreed.

I think if you didn't know our story, the two of us would have appeared awkward on that first date. Literally nothing happened! We just sat across from each other and smiled. When the check came, I was more than happy to pay the bill. I was more than happy to have driven seven hours by myself to get there. It was worth it because I was with *her*, and I didn't have to get anything from her because spending time together was enough to be satisfied. That probably sounds really cheesy, but it's true!

Oftentimes, that's what authentic worship looks like. We are present, and we give our whole selves just because it's good to be in the same room with God, just because we want to honor Him. Whatever the cost, He's always worth it! It's easy to get the concept of worship backwards. Often we go into worship because we want to receive something from God, but worship is about giving honor and praise to Him regardless whether or not we receive any tangible benefit from it. At its core, worship is supposed to be sacrificial. It's meant to cost us something.

In any relationship, when our expectations are off, it usually leads to disappointment. It is no different with God. Sometimes the Church makes the mistake of setting up the wrong expectations, expecting everyone to *feel* something as we sing and praise God together, but not everyone does, certainly not all the time. That can leave individuals who don't feel emotional during a worship service with some sense of inadequacy, like there must be something wrong with them because they don't seem to get what everyone else gets. Even worse, not receiving anything during worship can cause people to doubt that what we're doing together is even real at all. You might feel like "the emperor has no clothes" if you look around and can't see the reality that everyone else seems to see.

So, some people stop singing. They check their phones during their church's worship times or let their minds wander to things that seem more interesting. Some people begin to doubt their faith entirely. Sadly, that's where my friend Matt ended up several months later, having a complete crisis of faith, unable to discern whether anything he said he believed in was real or not.

If what I'm describing is a familiar scenario, for your entire life or even just through a certain season, I want to reassure you: it's okay! God is not angry with you. He's not hiding from you or withholding Himself from you to taunt you! Most of us go through seasons where we sense the ebb and flow of our emotions during worship.

King David (probably the ultimate worship songwriter!) certainly went through his ups and downs. Most people remember the 23rd Psalm; you know… "The Lord is my Shepherd…" It's amazing! I've written more than one song based around that Psalm. However, let's jump back one and look at Psalm 22:

> My God, my God, why have You forsaken me?
> Why are You so far from my deliverance
> and from my words of groaning?
> My God, I cry by day, but You do not answer,
> by night, yet I have no rest.
> Psalm 22: 1-2 (HCSB)

Clearly David isn't having the best day. He is not "feeling it." His life had a plethora of low points, but this was obviously one of the worst. Rather than put on a happy face and fake it or forget about God entirely, even though he felt abandoned, David poured out honesty before God. In so many words, David said, "God I don't feel you right now." But look where this goes:

> But You are holy,

> enthroned on the praises of Israel.
> Our fathers trusted in You;
> they trusted, and You rescued them.
> They cried to You and were set free;
> they trusted in You and were not disgraced.
> Psalm 22:3-5 (HCSB)

David turns to the reason for his praise: God Himself. He knows who God is because he recalls what God has done. One of the best things we can do to bolster our faith is continually hold testimonies within our vision. It grows easier to trust God for breakthrough when we recall what He has already done.

> But I am a worm and not a man,
> scorned by men and despised by people.
> Everyone who sees me mocks me;
> they sneer and shake their heads:
> "He relies on the Lord;
> let Him rescue him;
> let the Lord deliver him,
> since He takes pleasure in him."
> Psalm 22:6-8 (HCSB)

Yikes! David's confidence is almost completely shot. It seems that the more he trusts in God, the worse things get. People are noticing, and they're mocking him. It makes him feel…worthless. But remember, this is a Psalm, a hymn of devotion to God. Rather than hide his pain or let it consume him, David lays it all before God, not in a way that makes demands on God but pledging his devotion regardless.

Where he ends up is remarkable considering the bitter anguish he was feeling:

> I will proclaim Your name to my brothers;
> I will praise You in the congregation.
> You who fear Yahweh, praise Him!
> All you descendants of Jacob, honor Him!
> All you descendants of Israel, revere Him!

> For He has not despised or detested
> the torment of the afflicted.
> He did not hide His face from him
> but listened when he cried to Him for help.
> I will give praise in the great congregation
> because of You;
> I will fulfill my vows
> before those who fear You.
> Psalm 22:22-25 (HCSB)

This is authentic worship! At a moment when David feels completely abandoned by God and faces persecution for his faith, he resolves to not only worship God privately but also proclaim His name publicly. David has counted the cost and decided to give his all regardless. At his bleakest moment, David's song captures the essence of worship.

It's the same heart that led Shadrach, Meshach, and Abednego to stand boldly before the evil King Nebuchadnezzar and refuse to worship his golden idol. Under the threat of being burned alive, they made one of the most powerful declarations of loyalty in the Bible:

> If the God we serve exists, then He can rescue us
> from the furnace of blazing fire, and He can rescue
> us from the power of you, the king. But even if He
> does not rescue us, we want you as king to know
> that we will not serve your gods or worship the gold
> statue you set up.
> Daniel 3:17-18 (HCSB)

"But even if He does not rescue us..." Just like David, these men of God knew that faithfulness to Him was worth any price they might pay, even if they got nothing out of it.

But I have some very good news: God *did* meet Shadrach, Meshach, and Abednego in the fire. He *did* rescue them. God *did* rescue David from his moment of calamity. And He absolutely shows up when we worship Him! Just look back at the beginning of Psalm 22:

> But You are holy,
> enthroned on the praises of Israel.
> Psalm 22:3 (HCSB)

Some translations of this verse say, "You *inhabit* the praises of Israel." **Worship is where God chooses to keep company.** When we worship, we welcome God to sit on the throne of our hearts. Authentic worship says, "Have Your will and Your way in my situation. I will praise you with much, or I will praise you with little." Our praises shouldn't dictate to God how He should show up on our behalf because that puts *us* on the throne. Instead, like David, we bring our deepest longings before God and surrender them to His holiness. In that place of vulnerability, we have tremendous hope that God will move on our behalf because, over and over in Scripture, that's what He promises to do. Remember, this is a victorious surrender!

God is your ever-present help in your time of need (Psalm 46). He is your refuge (Psalm 16). He listens to you closely, answers when you call, and protects you as closely as one protects the pupil of his own eye (Psalm 17). He delights in you (Psalm 149)! He chases after you with goodness and mercy (Psalm 23). I could go on and on, just from the Psalms, and the entire Bible is full of incredible promises about God's kindness and generosity.

It is vital that we hold God's goodness as an unshakeable foundation of our faith, a cornerstone of our theology. Sacrificial worship comes naturally when we trust in His warm affection for us. It is out of that perfect goodness that God promises His presence to us. Whether we feel anything or not, as we pour out our devotion to Him, He inhabits our praise. We can rest in that promise and not have to worry about the fickleness of emotions. He graces us with His presence because He loves us. He will not abandon you. The goodness of God cannot be overstated; it cannot be exaggerated.

The awesome presence of God is the result of His benevolence. God, who has an infinite capacity for relationship, is more interested in spending time with us than we are with Him (nothing could ever tip the scales in that equation). He is always there, waiting for you to enter communion with Him.

God is not insecure. He isn't needy of compliments. The reason He so fervently desires your praise is that it's yours to give. No one else in the universe could give Him your praise because you are uniquely, fearfully, and wonderfully made. He desires your worship because He loves you, the amazing individual reading this book right now! Furthermore, the reason He *commands* you to praise Him is that He wants what's best for you, and God knows that there is nothing better than Himself.

You see, when it's all said and done, we become like what we worship. As I said in the previous chapter, we are all hardwired to worship *something*, and worshiping anything other than God diminishes us. Look what it says in Psalm 115:

> Their idols are silver and gold,
> made by human hands.
> They have mouths but cannot speak,
> eyes, but cannot see.
> They have ears but cannot hear,
> noses, but cannot smell.
> They have hands but cannot feel,
> feet, but cannot walk.
> They cannot make a sound with their throats.
> Those who make them become just like them,
> as are all who trust in them.
> Psalm 115:4-8 (HCSB)

When we worship dead things, we become like them, spiritually mute, blind, and powerless. However, when we worship the Living God, we are filled with His likeness.

> But we all, with unveiled face, beholding as in a
> mirror the glory of the Lord, are being transformed
> into the same image from glory to glory, just as from

> the Lord, the Spirit.
> 2 Corinthians 3:18 (NASB)

My dear friend and mentor Bishop Dan Scott has reminded me often that to "behold" literally means to "hold with one's being." That is truly what worship is: to wrap your life around the life of God.

So, what should we do when our worship feels empty? How should we respond when others around us seem to be connecting with God in a way that we are not? Perhaps the best thing we can do is celebrate their victories as we would our own. Remember, as Christians, we are a family, and when one person finds connection to the Father, we share in the blessings they receive. The key that unlocks these blessings is gratitude. Rather than respond with jealousy, despair, cynicism, or apathy, resolve in your heart to respond to God with thanksgiving.

Ultimately, the challenge of sacrificial worship revolves around whether or not we actually believe that God is as good as He says He is. Remember, we see the evidence of who God is in the things He does. But rather than sit on our hands and wait for Him to do something new, we need only look back and remember what He has already done.

When we look at the life of Jesus, we see perfectly the character of the Father (John 14:9). So, let's look with fresh eyes at a story most of us have heard many times over. Let's *behold* Him, so that we might become like Him:

> Then Jesus came with them to a place called Gethsemane, and He told the disciples, "Sit here while I go over there and pray." Taking along Peter and the two sons of Zebedee, He began to be sorrowful and deeply distressed. Then He said to them, "My soul is swallowed up in sorrow — to the point of death. Remain here and stay awake with Me." Going a little farther, He fell facedown and

> prayed, "My Father! If it is possible, let this cup pass from Me. Yet not as I will, but as You will."
> Matthew 36:36-39 (HCSB)

Just like Shadrach, Meshach, and Abednego, Jesus willingly placed His life in the hands of the Father. Jesus presented His fervent desire to the Father but did not dictate the outcome. At Gethsemane, He modeled the ultimate attitude of sacrifice: resolving to follow the will of God, even though it would cost Him everything.

When you find yourself in the middle of adversity, you are actually closer to Christ than you might realize. You are united with Him in suffering (Philippians 3:10). It is there, in your weakness, that you will encounter His perfect strength, and His power will rest upon you and reside inside of you (2 Corinthians 12:9).

Not much later, after a complete mockery of justice, Jesus was brutally beaten and tortured. He did not fight back or make appeals for Himself. Although He certainly had the authority to do so, He did not call down the armies of Heaven to consume the soldiers that nailed His hands and feet to the cross. Instead He forgave the people who perpetrated this great injustice.

Jesus gave Himself willingly, and as He endured physical pain on the cross, He also experienced the brunt of forlornness, the anguish of feeling abandoned by His Father.

> From noon until three in the afternoon darkness came over the whole land. About three in the afternoon Jesus cried out with a loud voice, "Elí, Elí, lemá sabachtháni?" that is, "My God, My God, why have You forsaken Me?"
> Matthew 27:45-47 (HCSB)

"My God, my God, why have you forsaken me?" Sound familiar? Psalm 22 is not just an intimate look into David's relationship with God during a time of deep sorrow (though it is certainly that). It's also one of the most profound Old

Testament prophecies of what Jesus would endure on the cross.

As Jesus looked down from the cross and saw the Roman soldiers gambling for his clothes, the words of David's powerful Psalm were resounding in His heart:

> My strength is dried up like baked clay;
> my tongue sticks to the roof of my mouth.
> You put me into the dust of death.
> For dogs have surrounded me;
> a gang of evildoers has closed in on me;
> they pierced my hands and my feet.
> I can count all my bones;
> people look and stare at me.
> They divided my garments among themselves,
> and they cast lots for my clothing.
> Psalm 22:15-18 (HCSB)

"My God, my God, why have You forsaken me." Those words would not have been unfamiliar to the Pharisees who, less than 24 hours earlier, sought out false witnesses to lie about Jesus before the Roman authorities, beat Him with their fists, and blasphemed Him. The author of Hebrews wrote powerfully about this very moment:

> But we do see Jesus — made lower than the angels for a short time so that by God's grace He might taste death for everyone — crowned with glory and honor because of His suffering in death. For in bringing many sons to glory, it was entirely appropriate that God — all things exist for Him and through Him — should make the source of their salvation perfect through sufferings.
> For the One who sanctifies and those who are sanctified all have one Father. That is why Jesus is not ashamed to call them brothers, saying:
> **I will proclaim Your name to My brothers;**

> ***I will sing hymns to You in the congregation.***
> Hebrews 2:9-12 (HCSB)

Those last two lines that I've highlighted, the lines that Hebrews says Jesus himself sang, are also another quote from Psalm 22.

You see, when Jesus shouted out, "My God, my God, why have you forsaken me?" he wasn't just quoting the first line of Psalm 22, He was living out the the Psalm in its entirety. **It wasn't just a cry of despair, it was worship.**

Worship begins and ends with Jesus. We worship Him for who He is, and we see the evidence of who He is in what He has done. Our sacrificial worship is modeled on the sacrifice that Jesus made of Himself, and we know that He is worthy because He did not exclude Himself from what He's called us to do. Instead, He made Himself like us so that we might become like Him.

Jesus leads our worship by example, and He has already completed our worship in every way that we fall short. Our inherited privilege is to join our worship with His, and in doing so, we reap a harvest of perfect love that only He could deserve. The nearness to God we experience in worship, the blessings we receive in this life, and the glory of His presence are all His unmerited gift to us for something we could not possibly do on our own. They give us all the more reason to respond to Him with our entire being:

> Holy, holy, holy is the Lord of Hosts;
> His glory fills the whole earth.
> Isaiah 6:3 (HCSB)

6 UNDIVIDED

Is it possible to write a book or a sermon about worship and not talk about King David? When I was younger, I used to scratch my head at all the worship leaders and pastors who singled out David as their favorite person in the Bible. David, who was no doubt a remarkable man, was an enigma to me. Obviously, he gave us the Psalms, the foundation for virtually all of worship music, but he was also riddled with devastating character flaws.

David was a strange walking contradiction of things: a shepherd, poet, musician, prophet, warrior, servant, king. At times, when it seemed like all was going wrong, he embodied seemingly super-human devotion to God. Other times, when it seemed like things were going well for him, he flagrantly disobeyed God (and ruined more than a few lives in the process). Still, I have always been taught that God's grace and love stretch beyond our mistakes, even big ones, and I chalked up David as an amazing example of God's unmerited goodness. But favorite Bible character? No, David was not mine.

Stranger still, God singled out David as "a man after My own heart." How is it that Jesus, who is the Son of God, chose also to be known as the Son of David? I can't imagine a higher honor being bestowed on anyone! Yet, when I read about David's life, I saw a man who seemed to invent ways to offend God, even after God lavishly blessed him. When I read the Psalms, many of them seemed awful and dreary to me, full of harsh, sometimes violent language. I always liked the good parts of David's life but wrinkled my nose at David's rough edges. What was it about this man that so many Christian leaders I admire are attracted to…that God Himself seems to attracted to?

As I have grown older and reread David's story and the Psalms countless times, I've grown increasingly fond of him. Many of his character flaws, I've come to recognize as similar to my own; and with that recognition, my offense at his sins has turned largely into gratitude for God's faithfulness toward him. From my vantage point today, David seems like some sort of Old Testament prototype of what a New Testament disciple might look like. For every mistake he made, we find David running back into God's arms, throwing himself upon grace he knew he was unworthy of. David spent so much time in God's presence, studying God's Word, that he gained revelations about God's nature that most other Old Testament figures seem to have missed. One of the biggest of these is the fact that God receives glory in extending grace and redeeming a broken past.

> He renews my life;
> He leads me along the right paths
> for His name's sake.
> Psalm 23:3 (HCSB)

For *His* name's sake. God receives glory in a renewed life, in a restored soul. He leads us into a life of righteousness because doing so exalts His name. Time and again, when David would fall, God would restore him; and God was glorified in the restoration. David would return to the comfort of the Holy Spirit's presence, even more steadfast than before, fully throwing himself into a life of worship. The thought of being without the Holy Spirit because of sin anguished David:

> God, create a clean heart for me
> and renew a steadfast spirit within me.
> Do not banish me from Your presence

> or take Your Holy Spirit from me.
> Restore the joy of Your salvation to me,
> and give me a willing spirit.
> Then I will teach the rebellious Your ways,
> and sinners will return to You.
> Psalm 51:10-13 (HCSB)

That passage has always amazed me because David clearly had an intimacy with the Holy Spirit that was unusual for a person under the Old Covenant. This was over a thousand years before God poured out the Holy Spirit in Acts 2. David's life was a foretaste of what God has now opened up to all believers.

But what was it that made David so special to God? I think we might have a big clue in Psalm 86. In it, David pleads with God for mercy and forgiveness. Confident that God is compassionate, David resolves ahead of time to respond to God's rescue:

> Teach me Your way, Yahweh,
> and I will live by Your truth.
> **Give me an undivided mind to fear Your name.**
> **I will praise You with all my heart, Lord my God**,
> and will honor Your name forever.
> For Your faithful love for me is great,
> and You deliver my life from the depths of Sheol.
> Psalm 86:11-13 (HCSB)

That simple prayer "give me an undivided mind" has been ringing in my ears for years now. Some translations say "unite my heart" or "make my heart undivided." David knew that although God covered him with righteousness, he still struggled to keep himself from acting in ways that dishonored God. That dichotomy rings true in my own life. It's a struggle that the Apostle Paul echoed in the New Testament:

> For in my inner self I joyfully agree with God's law.

> But I see a different law in the parts of my body, waging war against the law of my mind and taking me prisoner to the law of sin in the parts of my body. What a wretched man I am! Who will rescue me from this dying body? I thank God through Jesus Christ our Lord! So then, with my mind I myself am a slave to the law of God, but with my flesh, to the law of sin.
> Romans 7:22-25 (HCSB)

Paul, on this side of the cross, had perspective that David could not have had to recognize that his true identity resided in Christ and not the desires of his body. The Christian life we live day by day might be described as such: a spirit that is at once fully alive in Christ and a soul (mind, will, emotions) that is still in process. That is why Paul urges us in Philippians 2:12 to "work out your own salvation with fear and trembling." Your spirit was fully saved when you surrendered your life to Jesus; your soul is being saved day by day as you pursue Jesus; and your body will be saved when Jesus returns.

"Give me an undivided mind *to fear your name.*" David and Paul both spoke about the fear of the Lord. To many, fearing God seems like a strange concept. If God is supremely good, why should we fear or tremble? Aren't those two ideas incongruent? Not really. The English word "fear" is really too weak to carry the full meaning of the Hebrew or Greek, but we can approach understanding by digging a little deeper. Psalm 2 actually describes a "reverential awe" and "rejoicing with trembling." Psalm 112 says, "Happy is the man who fears the Lord."

Let me describe it this way: Last year, I had the privilege of leading a group of high school students on a mission trip here in my home town of Nashville. Throughout the day, the students worked at different service projects across the city: distributing food to the homeless, caring for adults with special needs, etc.

One of the students, Caleb, was a very accomplished mandolin player. His musical heroes were different from most of his fellow high school students. Instead of pop stars or rock bands, he got excited about bluegrass musicians (many of whom live here in Nashville). Caleb's practice routines were rigid and included playing Bach solo violin concertos on mandolin to improve his technical dexterity.

On the last day here in Nashville, the students were given some free time to explore the city, and Caleb's youth leader took him to visit Carter Vintage Guitars, a shop here in town that specializes in some of the finest (and most expensive) stringed instruments in the world. This place is as much museum as it is a functioning musical instruments shop.

There are instruments in Carter Vintage Guitars that live in glass cases because of their extreme value, and very few people get permission to take them out and play them. Several of these instruments are vintage mandolins hand-made and signed by legendary luthier Lloyd Loar, and they are the most sought-after mandolins in the world—the bluegrass version of a Stradivarius violin. Caleb went into the shop just to gaze at a Loar mandolin behind glass, to admire it and dream about it (and experience the sticker shock of seeing such a small instrument with a price tag of over $250,000!).

That day, however, was special because a serious buyer came in, and the service staff at Carter Vintage unlocked the glass case and let the man play the Loar. Caleb stood in awe, listening to the customer try out one of the most valuable instruments he had ever seen before. Finishing up, the man was just about to hand the Loar mandolin back to the store staff person when he paused.

He turned to Caleb and said, "I heard you playing Bach on some of the other mandolins in here. Do you want to try it?" He held the Loar out, offering it to Caleb, and Caleb was completely astonished!

I saw Caleb about an hour after he played the Lloyd Loar mandolin, and he was still breathless. "I could barely play the thing!" he said. "My hands were shaking so bad. I was terrified! My hands are still shaking...look!" He held up both hands and they were trembling with excitement that hadn't subsided. "I think I could cry if I thought about it too much! I just went in to look at it. I never dreamed I'd hear somebody else play it, let alone play it myself! I can't even believe that just happened."

Caleb was on Cloud 9 for hours after that experience. At some point, the Holy Spirit whispered to my heart, one of those bright "Aha!" moments. I turned to Caleb and told him, "Caleb, you know that feeling you're experiencing right now? That might be the best metaphor I've ever heard to describe 'the fear of the Lord.'"

Caleb's literal terrified trembling wasn't horror at the threat of pain or punishment. It wasn't dismay or dread. It was awe so deep that it physically shook him, the response to holding something so valuable, when he knew he was unqualified to do so. It was deep, vision-blurring, heart-pumping, lump-in-your-throat reverence. And it was beautiful!

The fear of the Lord is both an end goal and the means by which we live with an undivided heart. When we approach the throne of God with the awesome awareness that He is worthy beyond words and powerful beyond comprehension, we begin to catch new glimpses of His character. With every new glimpse of God, trembling wonder washes over our being again, and we find yet another reason to treasure His presence. Worship begets revelation, and revelation begets even more worship. Deep calls unto deep.

King David recognized that one of the biggest threats to such an ongoing life cycle of worship and wonder is a divided heart. I believe that his enduring pursuit of a unified heart and mind before God is one of the biggest reasons God so magnificently honored David's life. While certainly falling prey to tragic stumbles along the way, David relentlessly chased after the presence of God, and recognized that God's goodness and mercy were also chasing after him. His lifelong ambition was to build a temple for the Lord in which unending worship would be offered up day and night, a public dream that was birthed in David's private communion with God.

As Christians, we serve God and worship Him out of two primary components of our life: what is visible and what is invisible. The visible is what other people see and largely makes up how we are perceived and evaluated. It includes spiritual gifts, natural talents, accomplishments, and even one's anointing. These are the things for which we get patted on the back and congratulated and are usually that which we notice and admire in others. We notice when a pastor delivers a stirring sermon or when a worship leader sings a song exceptionally well. We are thankful when a teacher's ability to communicate complicated ideas shines above the rest of his or her colleagues. We admire and aspire to the accomplishments of saintly men and women.

What's important to recognize about your visible worship is that it is largely made up of things that are free gifts from God. God is the giver of talents and spiritual gifts. God is the one who anoints us for service. God is the one with authority and sovereignty to see that our efforts succeed or fail. He gives the singer a voice. He gives the teacher insight. He gives the pastor leadership ability. He gives the prophet vision. He anoints the politician for public service. Whatever your career or office, however you've been called to live your life of worship, God is the one who gives you the tools with which to succeed.

That does not, however, diminish the value of visible worship. What is visible is vitally important and often is what draws unbelievers into faith. When our visible worship is divided from our private lives, the Gospel message gets compromised. A divided heart is what leads a person to show up to church week after week and walk out the door unchanged, and that kind of division is easy for the world to spot.

We see it all too often don't we? Perhaps you've even been

guilty of it yourself…I know I have. At church, we wear our church faces. At work, we wear our work faces. And when we're around our friends, we wear the coolest, most likable faces we can muster. Our lives get compartmentalized. Faith becomes "personal" and privatized and rarely has any impact on daily life. When our hearts are divided, rarely do we talk about our relationship with Jesus with anyone outside the four walls of church. *We wouldn't want to make anybody feel awkward.*

Worse yet, a divided heart can chain us to secret sins and lead us into the bondage of cyclical shame. It is the weak point at which Satan launches his most insidious weapons. The divided heart is what leads great men and women of God into public scandal. It's the reason the couple who seemed to have it all together suddenly find their marriage falling apart. It's what causes well-meaning Christians to sing their hearts out in church but at home, behind closed doors, wrestle with substance abuse, eating disorders, pornography, and promiscuity. Satan jumps on these sins like a lion devouring a wounded animal and uses them to further drive a wedge in our hearts.

Like David and like Paul, we must recognize these weaknesses of the flesh for what they are, and rather than fall prey to the brutal death spiral of sin and shame, throw ourselves fully onto the mercy and kindness of God. His kindness will lead us to repentance (Romans 2), and repentance will lead us back into fellowship with Him where He brings restoration and redemption even to our worst mistakes.

> Be gracious to me, Lord,
> for I call to You all day long.
> Bring joy to Your servant's life,
> because I turn to You, Lord.
> For You, Lord, are kind and ready to forgive,
> rich in faithful love to all who call on You.
> Lord, hear my prayer;
> listen to my plea for mercy.
> I call on You in the day of my distress,
> for You will answer me.

Psalm 86:3-7 (HCSB)

Most of us really like the idea of Jesus being our Savior, but making him Lord over our lives? That's a little different. Left unchecked, however, a divided heart slowly erodes away our fear of God. Awestruck wonder turns into going through the motions. Trembling joy turns into casual compromise. Thanksgiving turns into entitlement. We stop holding God with our entire being and begin holding Him at arm's length.

Throughout the Bible, we read stern warnings and admonitions for those who worship with a divided heart and mind. Jesus fiercely challenged the Pharisees, whose lives consisted almost entirely of *visible* worship, with the words of the prophet Isaiah:

> He answered them, "Isaiah prophesied correctly about you hypocrites, as it is written:
> **These people honor Me with their lips, but their heart is far from Me.**
> They worship Me in vain,
> teaching as doctrines the commands of men.
> Disregarding the command of God, you keep the tradition of men."
> Mark 7:6-8 (HCSB)

While our visible acts of worship are not without their importance, what Jesus is after is something deeper, and that is the component of our lives that is largely invisible to the rest of the world. Very often, visible worship costs us very little and can serve as an easy cover for spiritual emptiness. But God isn't after empty gestures; He's after your heart.

David learned this vital lesson early on in life, and when he fell into his deepest sin, he offered God not a sacrifice but the entirety of his heart:

> Save me from the guilt of bloodshed, God,
> the God of my salvation,
> and my tongue will sing of Your righteousness.

> Lord, open my lips,
> and my mouth will declare Your praise.
> You do not want a sacrifice, or I would give it;
> **You are not pleased with a burnt offering.**
> **The sacrifice pleasing to God is a broken spirit.**
> God, You will not despise a broken and humbled heart.
> In Your good pleasure, cause Zion to prosper;
> build the walls of Jerusalem.
> Then You will delight in righteous sacrifices,
> whole burnt offerings;
> then bulls will be offered on Your altar.
> Psalm 51:14-19 (HCSB)

It's not that God doesn't want our visible worship, but that in order for it to be acceptable to Him (and transformative for us), our visible worship must live on top of the foundation of a clean heart and a right spirit. It's the part of us that only God truly sees.

Our invisible worship is made up of our character. It includes our love for Jesus, our pursuit of Him, our faith, our integrity, and our virtue. Behind closed doors, with all the cards on the table, the essence of your true self—that is what God is after.

If our visible worship is largely made up of what are free gifts from God, our invisible worship is where we will find the things that take careful cultivation and maintenance. Our invisible worship is where communion with the Holy Spirit really flourishes, and time spent with the Spirit always yields spiritual fruit:

> But the fruit of the Spirit is love, joy, peace, patience, kindness, goodness, faith, gentleness, self-control. Against such things there is no law. Now those who belong to Christ Jesus have crucified the flesh with its passions and desires. Since we live by

the Spirit, we must also follow the Spirit.
Galatians 5:22-25 (HCSB)

Notice something interesting here: When Paul talks about the *gifts* of the Spirit in 1 Corinthians 12, they are many and varied from person to person. However, when talking about the *fruit* of the Spirit, it is singular. Love, joy, peace, patience, kindness, goodness, faith, gentleness, and self-control: they're all one fruit! Much like an apple is simultaneously sweet, tart, crunchy, and juicy; the fruit of the Spirit is simultaneously all of those virtues. We are not assigned each our own fruit, some people being patient and others being joyful. No! Spending time, devoting ourselves to the Holy Spirit's work, should yield all of these Heavenly character traits.

In our lives, any deficiency in one aspect of the fruit of the Spirit is remedied simply by deeper communion with the Holy Spirit. It doesn't come from striving or trying harder within your own ability but from being empowered by the Spirit's ability and co-laboring with Him to build on the foundation that is Jesus (1 Corinthians 3).

You see, the fruit of anything is simply more of itself. The fruit of an apple tree is an apple, which contains in itself the ability to reproduce more of its kind. The fruit of a tomato plant is a tomato, which contains in itself the ability to reproduce more tomatoes. As we offer up our whole heart through communion with God, He doesn't just give us pleasant character traits; He gives us Himself! He is Joy. He is Love. He is Peace. As you give yourself to Him, He continues to pour more of Himself into you! He is inexhaustible and completely satisfying! There is always room in Him to grow deeper roots and richer fruit.

What God asks from us is simply that we surrender to Him the soil of our hearts, allowing Him to cultivate our character, to plow where He wishes, to pull out the weeds that might choke out His fruit, and to keep us fed and watered by his Word and Spirit. **God wants from you what only you can give Him: your love and your devotion. Anyone can give a sacrifice, but only you can give Him your heart**

behind the sacrifice.

King Saul, David's predecessor, looked the part of a king. The book of 1 Samuel says he was strong, handsome and stood head and shoulders above everyone else. He had all the outward markers of what the Israelites thought they wanted in a king. But he had a jealous heart, needy for the applause of others, and he was disobedient to God's instruction. In 1 Samuel 15, God instructed Saul to destroy all of the plunder from his battle with the Amalekites, but Saul rebelled, destroying only the worthless things but keeping the best sheep, rams, and cattle alive.

When the prophet Samuel confronted Saul about his disobedience, Saul's excuse was to say that he intended to use those choice animals for sacrifice to God! Look at Samuel's reply:

> Then Samuel said:
> Does the Lord take pleasure in burnt offerings
> and sacrifices as much as in obeying the Lord?
> Look: to obey is better than sacrifice,
> to pay attention is better than the fat of rams.
> For rebellion is like the sin of divination,
> and defiance is like wickedness and idolatry.
> Because you have rejected the word of the Lord,
> He has rejected you as king.
> I Samuel 15:22-23 (HCSB)

God wasn't after Saul's burnt offerings. He wanted Saul's heart. From that moment, God turned His attention away from Saul and onto David, a man who would pursue God with his whole heart for his entire life.

You see, sacrifice, even in the Old Testament, has always been a reflection of God's grace toward the contrite heart. It's easy to miss, but once you start looking, the evidence for this is readily apparent. In Exodus and Leviticus, even as all the rules for worship and sacrifice are being laid out, we see a thread of grace all throughout. It wasn't that the presentation of a lamb somehow paid the price for the sins of Israel. After all, in Leviticus 5, God instructed people who couldn't afford a lamb to bring two doves. And if they couldn't afford two doves, they should bring some grain instead. Even that early on, God was laying the foundation for the story of His grace.

From his time spent in God's presence, David gained astonishing revelation of God's nature. In an era when the Law of Moses was considered to be the pathway to salvation, David realized that it was actually faith in God Himself that saved. The Apostle Paul affirmed David's tremendous revelation in Romans:

> David also speaks of the blessing of the man God credits righteousness to apart from works:
> How joyful are those whose lawless acts are forgiven and whose sins are covered!
> How joyful is the man
> the Lord will never charge with sin!
> Romans 4:6-8 (HCSB)

Paul here is referencing David's Psalm 32, which was written 28 generations before Christ came and revealed the nature of grace through faith to all the world. But because of David's undivided heart for the Lord, God revealed Himself in ways that were truly awe inspiring!

We know now that there is only one Lamb whose sacrifice could pay off the debt of sin, and that is Jesus Himself. Even in the Old Testament, worship wasn't really about the sacrifice itself. It was about presenting a repentant heart before God, and the sacrifice was both a symbol of giving God the best of what you have to offer and a prophetic picture looking forward to Jesus.

If you go all the way back to the earliest sacrifices of the Bible, you'll see that this is true. We have little Scriptural basis to think that Cain's first fruits were somehow materially inferior to Abel's. Each of the brothers brought the harvest of his labor (Genesis 4). What we do know, however, is that

Cain's heart was not in his offering, and that is why God did not accept it. Cain was divided. He didn't bring his best to God—that is, not just the fruit of his labor but his entire being.

Think about it for a moment: What use does God have for fruit and lambs? For that matter, what use does He have for singing or dancing or lifting hands? God needs nothing, but He desires the entirety of your affection and devotion. He desires for His children to pursue Him both in public and private. He wants us to live a life permeated by the Gospel, with one mind and one heart constantly in communion with Him.

It's all too easy to compartmentalize our lives, dividing our attention and devotion between God, family, friends, work, etc.. But devotion to God should permeate all corners of our hearts and every aspect of our lives. The Bible tells us that the Apostle Paul earned his living by making tents. But, for Paul, tent making was not a separate part of life from his calling to preach the Gospel. In Acts 19, we see that the work aprons he wore during his labor were soaked in God's presence, and when they were brought to the sick, those who touched them were healed!

Rather than going to church to worship, we should arrive at church already worshiping! What would it be like if our congregational worship gatherings were merely a corporate exclamation point on daily routines already soaked in worship? I believe you would find every aspect of your life flourishing more fully, not just your Sunday church experience. This is because a whole life of worship, with an undivided heart and mind, has been God's plan all along. It's why God's affection toward King David is so evident in the Bible, because he modeled a unified heart throughout his life.

Are there areas of your life that have not been surrendered to God? Are there corners of your heart or routines of your mind that don't honor him? Loving God with your whole being takes effort, community, accountability, and vigilance. But the Holy Spirit is God's gift to you to help you along the way and continue to satisfy you as only God can. Remember, God said He will never leave you or forsake you (Deuteronomy 31:6). If you begin this journey and keep after Him, the Holy Spirit will guide you and keep your compass pointing true north!

Over the course of his life, King David learned this full well; and out of his total satisfaction in God, he gave us one of the most beautiful and profound passages in all of the Bible:

> The Lord is my shepherd;
> there is nothing I lack.
> He lets me lie down in green pastures;
> He leads me beside quiet waters.
> He renews my life;
> He leads me along the right paths
> for His name's sake.
> Even when I go through the darkest valley,
> I fear no danger,
> for You are with me;
> Your rod and Your staff — they comfort me.
> You prepare a table before me
> in the presence of my enemies;
> You anoint my head with oil;
> my cup overflows.
> Only goodness and faithful love will pursue me
> all the days of my life,
> and I will dwell in the house of the Lord
> as long as I live.
> Psalm 23 (HCSB)

You see, God doesn't just want all of your heart and mind because He's greedy. He wants all of you because He knows that only He can really satisfy you; and with Him, we have a feast! Satan tries to divide your heart with all manner of distractions and temptations, but all of those are simply counterfeits, temporary "fixes" that only create more brokenness. Jesus is the only thing good enough to quench your thirst and satisfy your hunger. He's the only one who can truly mend your torn heart, and He is lavish with Himself! As you give yourself to Him, He will never stop pouring Himself into you. And as He does, you will find yourself full to overflowing and begin pouring out rivers of life onto the people around you.

With unified hearts and minds, our visible expressions of worship take on new heights as our invisible worship grows deeper and deeper roots. The gifts of the Spirit are met with the fruit of the Spirit, and we become the kind of people who are so satisfied by God that we may begin feeding others from what He has grown in us. This life is attractive, and the world is hungry for what God has to offer!

7 THE SECRET PLACE

The Bible closes with a wedding ceremony, and marriage is one of the most profound living pictures God uses to describe the relationship between Jesus and the Church. No marriage can survive based solely on outward appearances, and public displays of affection are not a true measure of marital health. What person would honestly desire a marriage made up only of what happens in front of other people? Like all healthy personal relationships, marriages are formed from the inside out, through time and care, devotion and tenderness, trust and faith. True intimacy happens in secret, and it doesn't come from a one night stand.

Our relationship with the Bridegroom (Jesus) is no different. God desires the intimacy of an undivided heart more than just our outward displays of affection, and the road to an undivided heart begins in the secret place.

> "Whenever you pray, you must not be like the hypocrites, because they love to pray standing in the synagogues and on the street corners to be seen by people. I assure you: They've got their reward! But when you pray, go into your private room, shut your door, and pray to your Father who is in secret. And your Father who sees in secret will reward you.
> Matthew 6:5-6 (HCSB)

The greatest reward of pursuing the Father in the secret place is to be one with the Father Himself, just as Jesus was and prayed that we would be (John 17). Through intimacy with the Father, we learn what it truly means to be sons and daughters, co-heirs with Jesus. In that place, we find that the true essence of worship isn't in singing songs or doing charitable deeds (although we shouldn't neglect those things) but instead in giving Him our complete devotion, our undivided attention, and our sincerest affection. And Abba *loves* it! He is always waiting for us there in the secret place.

We learn from the many examples throughout David's Psalms that worship and prayer are attached at the hip. David's prayers are laid bare before God, never skimping on raw emotion, but rarely does he stray very far from exalting God for who He is and what He has done. Even in the direst of circumstances (as in Psalm 22 or Psalm 51), David does not let anguish overshadow his praise. Instead, he allows the presence of God to overshadow his pain, and resolutely pledges to worship God with his whole heart, even when his own future is uncertain. In that place of whole-hearted devotion, David found refuge in God's strength time and time again.

Before he became king, when David was on the run from King Saul, he described his longing for God as a deep thirst.

> God, You are my God; I eagerly seek You.
> I thirst for You;
> my body faints for You
> in a land that is dry, desolate, and without water.
> So I gaze on You in the sanctuary
> to see Your strength and Your glory.
> My lips will glorify You
> because Your faithful love is better than life.
> Psalm 63:1-5 (HCSB)

David knew that he would find God in his place of worship. There, he would drink in the strength and glory of God and cultivate it in his own heart through praise. Worship in the secret place was a habit that David formed early in his life, before anyone else noticed anything significant about him. Even his own father and the prophet Samuel overlooked him, but God looked deeper than appearances, to David's heart.

As David feasted on God's Word and the Holy Spirit's presence in the secret place, God endowed to him supreme confidence in His power. By the time he faced Goliath, his first public victory, David had already faced the lion and the bear in private. Knowing that the God of all creation was with him, he carried himself into battle with a swagger, with incredible God-confidence! Look at how he challenged Goliath:

> David said to the Philistine: "You come against me with a dagger, spear, and sword, but I come against you in the name of Yahweh of Hosts, the God of Israel's armies — you have defied Him. Today, the Lord will hand you over to me. Today, I'll strike you down, cut your head off, and give the corpses of the Philistine camp to the birds of the sky and the creatures of the earth. Then all the world will know that Israel has a God, and this whole assembly will know that it is not by sword or by spear that the Lord saves, for the battle is the Lord's. He will hand you over to us."
> I Samuel 17:45-47 (HCSB)

Boldness and strength to face giants are found in the secret place. Furthermore, our public service and worship are strengthened and grow deeper as we cultivate an undivided heart in the secret place. Throughout his life, whenever David was faithful to seek God in the secret place, God blessed his public efforts and protected him from harm. However, when David strayed from his pursuit of the Holy Spirit's presence, he stumbled publicly and exposed himself (and the nation of Israel) to severe hardship.

In the Gospels, we see Jesus frequently retreating to the secret place, away from the crowds, where He could spend time alone with His Father. Both before and after working miracles among thousands of people, Jesus would get away to commune alone with God. Before walking on water, Jesus was alone with the Father in the secret place (Matthew 14). Before delivering the demon possessed boy that the disciples could not help, Jesus was alone with the Father in the secret place (Matthew 17). Before going to the cross, Jesus was alone with the Father in the secret place (Matthew 26). Although Jesus routinely served great multitudes of people, He never allowed himself to burn out or grow dry. Likewise, we cannot expect to serve well in public if we're not taking the time to seek the Lord in private. No one can properly minister to the multitudes if he or she is not willing to be alone with an audience of One.

Jesus led by example, showing us that the secret place is where we find unity with the Father through the Holy Spirit. Jesus gave us the ultimate example of how to live with an undivided heart and mind. When we emerge from the secret place, we are not the same as we were before but are empowered to do the work of the Kingdom.

Time alone with God is vital for spiritual health and is a key component to discipleship. Following Jesus' example, we must not allow our identity, sense of accomplishment, or self confidence to be based on the validation we receive from other people. Instead, what God gives us during our times of devotion and communion with Him should be our driving force. With the Holy Spirit continually replenishing and growing us, there is no limit to what we can accomplish (Philippians 4:13).

Perhaps this concept is new to you, or perhaps you've tried in the past to develop a consistent devotional routine with God but have found it difficult to stick with. What does it look like to really commune with God in the secret place? How should we begin cultivating an undivided heart before God?

I have good news for you! God, who created you and

wired your brain, knows exactly how to communicate with you in a way that you will understand. God, who is the Inventor of relationships and is by His very nature relational, will not neglect a meaningful relationship with you. For this reason, God is not interested in formulaic rituals or meaningless routines. Remember, God mandated His altars not be made of identically-chiseled stones but of stones in their natural shape. Likewise, He loves to connect with you in a way that is the most sincere and honest for you. After all, He made you that way, and He loves His creation!

For the sake of simplicity (because one could write libraries on how to pursue God in the secret place), let's boil it down to its essence. At its core, all that is required is that you are present and God is present. God, for His part, will never fail to be present. So, that leaves us with simply the task of truly being present with Him.

It is perhaps best to begin with the comforting knowledge that God chose to relate to us through humanity and not solely as a lofty ideal (although among ideals, He is the loftiest!). God came as a man, as Jesus, who was the dear friend of James, John, Lazarus, Mary Magdalene, and Peter. Jesus described His affection for us as that of a mother hen, gathering her chicks under her wings (Matthew 23:37). Likewise, King David described resting in God's presence like a child resting on his mother (Psalm 131). We find in the Song of Songs and the book of Revelation the amazing imagery of Jesus loving us as intimately as a husband loves his bride. And, of course, God is our perfect Father, our Abba Daddy, in whose arms we find strength and comfort! We have these many representations throughout Scripture to reinforce the fact that with God we find perfect relationship.

As you retreat to a place of solitude before God, know that He is the Person your heart longs for. You may, as the Apostle John did, lay your head on Jesus' chest and know that His breath is upon you and His heart beats for you! You may run for shelter under the shadow if His wings. You may approach Him with the tenderest affection, like the bride in Song of Songs, saying "let Him kiss me!" You may run into

Abba's arms, like a little child and be held. Know that when you retreat to your quiet place, you are not alone! You have the Person of God present with you. You have His rapt attention and deepest love!

Your devotional life doesn't have to follow formulas or prescribed formats. These things can be an aid to guide your time and study of the Bible, but they're not requirements. What truly matters the most is that you make it a part of your routine to free yourself from distractions and spend time alone with God. Most people I have met start small (15 to 20 minutes) and allow their time with God to grow as their relationship with God deepens. If you cultivate it as a regular habit, you will likely soon find that these daily moments with God are more valuable than any other activity you might be participating in. Rather than it being a loss of otherwise productive time, God has a funny way of increasing your productivity throughout your day when you spend time with Him. It's a lot like tithing your money: when you give, God always manages to do more with your 90% than you could have done with 100%.

A healthy devotional life consists of more than just reading and praying. Worship (thanksgiving for who God is and what He has done), Bible reading, prayer, and simply listening for God's voice are all important aspects of time in the secret place. Remember, this isn't about checking off boxes of activities. It's an exchange of communication between you and the Person of God.

Since no two individuals are alike, no two people's quiet time with God looks quite the same. My wife keeps a journal and even paints during her devotional time. Many Christians around the world (including some of my closest mentors) use guides like the *Book of Common Prayer*'s "Daily Office" to help them direct their prayers and Scripture reading. Others enjoy topical devotional books or simply diving straight into the Bible and reading cover to cover. There are countless resources available to help you develop a deep and satisfying devotional life. Many of these are free and available anytime on the internet.

Personally, I try to spend time both in the morning and in the evening to set aside work and be with God. Monotonous routines tend to bore me rather quickly, and so I frequently cycle through short Bible reading plans rather than marathon year-long ones, often taking advantage of the many free options available on my smart phone. As I would with any friend, I allow my conversations with God to flow naturally, often picking up where we left off.

There have been times when I have read through the entire Bible quickly. Last year I did a 40-day whole-Bible reading plan that was intense and exhausting but so incredibly rich with insight! Other times, I have read through only a single book of the Bible in the same amount of time, allowing the text to wash over me in waves, slowly sinking in.

Remember, the Bible is not a mountain to be conquered. On the contrary, it is best when we allow the Scripture to conquer us! It's much more important to read one passage with understanding than to read quickly without letting anything absorb into your heart. Read at whatever pace your heart and mind can digest, and stop whenever you need to process it.

Your greatest asset when reading the Bible is the help of the Holy Spirit. All you need to do is ask, and God will begin highlighting passages that perfectly equip you for the tasks He has set before you. Before you begin reading, it's a good idea to stop and pray for God to open up the text to you as you read so that you might read with insight and sensitivity.

Last year, I led worship at an event with a fellow leader who I have looked up to since I was a kid. My parents owned his albums, and we frequently sang his songs in our church. This particular event was the first occasion I had ever spent any time with him in person, and he overflowed with joy and deep insight gained from years of time in the secret place with God.

One set of Scriptures he was particularly excited about, however, was perplexing to me. He read aloud these two passages with joyful anticipation he could barely contain:

> I will place the key of the House of David on his shoulder; what he opens, no one can close; what he closes, no one can open.
> Isaiah 22:22 (HCSB)

> Write to the angel of the church in Philadelphia: "The Holy One, the True One, the One who has the key of David, who opens and no one will close, and closes and no one opens says: I know your works. Because you have limited strength, have kept My word, and have not denied My name, look, I have placed before you an open door that no one is able to close.
> Revelation 3:7-8 (HCSB)

Those are the only two places in the Bible where the "Key of David" is mentioned, and my new friend was *very* excited about it.

"Isn't that amazing?" he asked. "It's so powerful! Jesus is the one who holds the key! What He opens, nobody can ever shut. What He shuts, nobody can ever open up again! Wow! It's just fantastic!"

"Okay," I thought. "I think I get it, but I obviously don't get it as much as he does!" I left the event unable to shake how captivated this worship leader was by the Key of David.

Returning home the next week, I started my devotional time by praying, "God, I need more revelation and understanding when I read. I don't really care if it's this Scripture or not…I'd love to be as excited about *any* verse as he was about the Key of David."

Then I worshiped God, spent time in prayer, and read the Bible. In the moment, I didn't seem to have any particular breakthrough or unusual insight into what I was reading, but I was thankful to have seen an example of how fulfilling it can be for someone who spends time reading God's Word.

Later that evening, I was leading worship for a 12-step group, made up of men and women in recovery for various substance abuse issues. As we sang and worshiped God together, I felt the Holy Spirit stirring my heart to speak up. The music grew quiet, and I began sharing what I felt like God was saying in the moment:

"God is here, and He is already completely victorious. Regardless which recovery step you're on, whether it's step 1 or step 12, you get to approach recovery from the position of total victory that Jesus already won on the cross."

And then what came out of my mouth stunned me! "The Bible says in Isaiah 22:22 and Revelation 3:7 that Jesus holds the Key of David; and what He opens, no one can shut. What He shuts, no one can open. Today, God can open your heart so wide to His healing and wholeness that no one could ever shut it again. He can slam the door on addiction so hard that nobody, not even you, could ever open it back up again!"

As I spoke, tears began to roll down the faces of the men and women in the room. It was a holy moment, and as we began singing together again, I stood in complete awe of God's amazing kindness and the power of His Word.

God breathed on that passage of Scripture during my time in the secret place, and I hadn't even realized it. But I got it when it mattered! And the insight from Heaven I received during my devotional time had a direct impact on my ministry to other people. Had I neglected to get alone and ask God for understanding, I don't believe I would have been prepared to do what God wanted me to do that night.

Even better, since praying that simple prayer, my every-day Bible reading has become a deeper well of insight and an even more precious time in God's presence. Stories that I have read countless times suddenly took on deeper levels of meaning as

God began opening my spiritual ears to hear His voice. Frequently, I finish my reading for the day in tears, and can only whisper aloud, "Thank you!" to the God who loves me enough to speak to my heart every day.

As with any friendship, not every conversation with the Lord begins the same way. Some days I begin by worshiping Him, sometimes silently in my heart but often as loudly and exuberantly as I would if I were leading a thousand people in worship. The countless worship songs and albums that are readily available frequently serve as a prompt for my own voice.

I recognize that it can be uncomfortable to do alone what might come more naturally when surrounded by a group of like minded people, all engaged in worship together. But I assure you, some of the most powerful worship experiences I have had in my life have been alone in my living room. When I first began worshiping God in private this way, I fully felt the awkwardness! My own voice suddenly sounded loud in my quiet house. My body felt stiff and uncomfortable. But something inside pushed me forward: if God is worthy of it when I'm with other people, He's worthy of all my worship when I am alone.

Give it a go! Put on some worship music or pull up a live stream of a worship service online (there are thousands of churches that stream and archive their services) and just worship Him. Sing loudly! Or sing quietly and reverently. Or sing silently from your heart. Sing your own song in your own words, or sing along with a song you already know. Let your affection for God be known! Join the angels in Heaven singing "Holy!" Kneel, sit, stand, lie on your face, dance, etc.. Give Him everything you have to offer. Remember, He inhabits your praise (Psalm 22). When we worship God with our whole heart, it always leads to communion with the Holy Spirit.

There are other days when it is God who starts the conversation and calls me to the secret place. I will feel the nudge of the Holy Spirit, not as a reminder of a task to be done, but as a friend inviting me into conversation with Him. He sometimes speaks to me about issues I'm currently facing or points me toward a certain passage in His Word, and I read carefully to understand what Jesus is saying to me.

Now, perhaps you've gotten to this point in the book and are wondering, *what do you mean, when you say things like "I feel the nudge of the Holy Spirit," or "I heard the Lord speak to my heart?"* That's an excellent question, and I'm glad you asked! Perhaps, in your own life, you've never experienced anything that you would call "hearing the voice of God." I want to encourage you that God *is* speaking, and you *do* have the ability to hear Him. I suspect that you may have already heard His voice and acted upon it without realizing it.

The Bible is full of examples of God speaking to people, both in the Old Testament and in the New Testament. Furthermore, throughout the over 2,000 years of recorded Church history, there are countless millions of accounts of God speaking to people clearly and accurately. God is not silent.

In John 10, Jesus says that we, His sheep, will hear and know the sound of His voice, and in John 14, He elaborates on the role the Holy Spirit plays in speaking to our hearts:

> And I will ask the Father, and **He will give you another Counselor to be with you forever. He is the Spirit of truth.** The world is unable to receive Him because it doesn't see Him or know Him. But you do know Him, because **He remains with you and will be in you**.
>
> "In a little while the world will see Me no longer, **but you will see Me.** Because I live, you will live too. In that day you will know that I am in My Father, you are in Me, and I am in you. The one who has My commands and keeps them is the one who loves Me.

And the one who loves Me will be loved by My Father. I also will love him and will reveal Myself to him."

Judas (not Iscariot) said to Him, "Lord, how is it You're going to reveal Yourself to us and not to the world? "

Jesus answered, "If anyone loves Me, he will keep My word. My Father will love him, and **We will come to him and make Our home with him.** The one who doesn't love Me will not keep My words. The word that you hear is not Mine but is from the Father who sent Me.
"I have spoken these things to you while I remain with you. **But the Counselor, the Holy Spirit — the Father will send Him in My name — will teach you all things and remind you of everything I have told you.**
John 14:16-25 (HCSB)

As His parting gift to His disciples, before He ascended into Heaven, Jesus breathed on them and said, "Receive the Holy Spirit" (John 20:22). This incredible gift manifested itself fully in Acts 2 in the upper room and again in Acts 4 when Peter and John prayed for boldness and again and again throughout the New Testament.

God chooses to speak in many different ways, as is evidenced throughout the entirety of Scripture. Often He speaks in the still small voice (1 Kings 19:5), which can be as simple as an impression, thought, or feeling in your heart that is from God (as the apostles and elders relied upon in Acts 15:28). Other times God speaks in a thunderous voice as He did to the Apostle Paul, knocking him off his horse and blinding him (Acts 9)! To Joseph, Daniel, Paul, John, Peter, and many others in the Bible, God spoke through dreams and visions. To the Queen of Sheba when she visited King Solomon, God spoke through beauty, art, and craftsmanship

(1 Kings 10). You may hear God's voice in a sermon or the advice of a friend. The Christmas star, the burning bush, the ephod, the hand writing on the wall, the voice of an angel. God uses whatever means might bring Him glory to speak to His children.

Most importantly, God uses His written Word, the Bible, to speak to us. **The Bible is the standard by which all other things are weighed. Nothing we hear or see or feel may ever contradict what God has already spoken in Scripture.** It is through the written Word that we learn God's character and commands, and by knowing those things we can more accurately evaluate what God speaks to us individually.

I'm well aware that many people (including myself) have been hurt by someone who claimed "God told me so." For this reason, many are understandably cautious about "hearing the voice of God." This is why it is so important that the Bible is the standard by which we judge any other word, no matter how convincing or emotional it might be. We also have the God-ordained Body of the Church and her leadership to help us interpret Scripture and discern matters that we may struggle to understand. It is virtually impossible to discern God's voice over time without knowing His character by studying what he says about Himself in the Bible.

However, it is also possible to know the Bible without truly knowing God or hearing His voice. The Pharisees knew the Scriptures backwards and forwards; yet Jesus, in John 5, rebuked them for not knowing God Himself. Today, there are many academics and leaders (both inside and outside the Church) who know the text and can recite the Bible, yet in their lives, we see no fruit of the Spirit. True discipleship cannot merely be an intellectual pursuit. Satan himself used Psalm 91 to tempt Jesus into committing suicide (Matthew 4), but Jesus, with the Holy Spirit resting upon Him, resisted the Devil's twisting of God's Word by relying on the full context of Scripture. Thus, we need both the Holy Spirit's voice and the written Word in order to best live life in the Kingdom of God.

Be encouraged! God created you, and He knows how your mind works. He knows exactly how to speak to you in a way that you will understand and recognize. I have found it best to allow God to choose whatever means He desires to speak and not try to dictate the particular method. If you struggle to discern or hear His voice, you need only ask for His help.

> "Whatever you ask in My name, I will do it so that the Father may be glorified in the Son. If you ask Me anything in My name, I will do it."
> John 14:13-14 (HCSB)

Jesus repeats this promise again in John 15 and in John 16. You may ask, just as King Solomon did in 1 Kings 3 for "a heart that listens" and discerns God's voice. God has already promised that He will answer your prayer. He is your loving Father, who delights in being connected to you (actually, even more than you love being connected to Him!), and He will not neglect to talk to you. If you ever find yourself feeling lonely or absent His voice, all you need to do is open the Bible and drink in.

In my own life, I have found the secret place with God is the best place to tune my heart to the Holy Spirit's voice. Often, as I worship the Lord or read the Bible, there comes a moment when I'm suddenly deeply aware of the presence of God. Sometimes, His presence draws me deeper into worship, and other times, it moves me to pray.

Years ago, God began bringing certain friends and family members to mind during my devotional time to pray for them. So, I started sending text messages to them after I was finished. Personally, I'm always encouraged when others let me know that they're praying for me, and I wanted to do the same. The messages were simple:

"Hey friend, just wanted you to know that you came to mind today, and I'm praying for you."

This became a regular practice, and I was amazed at how

frequently I would get a reply that said, "Wow! Your timing is perfect. I really needed to hear that today!" Of course, it was God's timing that was perfect and not mine.

This began happening more frequently, as the Holy Spirit would guide my thoughts. I got a little braver and began texting people longer messages, telling them more specifically *what* I was praying for them.

"Hey friend, you came to mind today. I wanted you to know that I'm praying for your work, that you would have strength to accomplish all the things on your plate. Praying that you would be encouraged and have creative ideas on how to solve any problems you run into along the way."

I was inspired by some of the prayers I read in Paul's letters to the early Church, how he exhorted them and encouraged:

> I never stop giving thanks for you as I remember you in my prayers. I pray that the God of our Lord Jesus Christ, the glorious Father, would give you a spirit of wisdom and revelation in the knowledge of Him. I pray that the perception of your mind may be enlightened so you may know what is the hope of His calling, what are the glorious riches of His inheritance among the saints, and what is the immeasurable greatness of His power to us who believe, according to the working of His vast strength.
> Ephesians 1:16-19 (HCSB)

How encouraging it must have been to receive one of Paul's letters, knowing that he was lifting you up in prayer! In 1 Thessalonians 5, Paul charges the Church with encouraging each other. I wanted to follow that example, and so I prayed for people's marriages and children, for their jobs and friendships, for their health and for their finances. Some situations I already knew about, and about others I knew nothing at all. Again and again, I received replies from friends who were amazed at how accurately I was praying for them, and sometimes they would send me testimonies of answered prayers.

Every time someone was encouraged and every time God answered a prayer, it became yet another opportunity to worship Him! Like King David modeled in the Psalms, worship led to prayer which led to more worship, and the cycle of thanksgiving and communion with God began to build.

What I didn't realize at the time is that I was actually practicing hearing the voice of God in a simple, practical way. In doing so, I learned to trust the Holy Spirit's guidance which has, over time, given me more courage to follow God's voice throughout all areas of my life.

The secret place is where we learn to unite our hearts and minds with the heart of God. It's a place of confession, adoration, repentance, intercession, and devotion to God's Word. Most of all, it's the place where we begin to step deeper into God's presence and His purpose for our lives. As I said before, each person's devotional life looks a little different from the next, but all of us must follow Jesus' example and get away from the crowds where we can be alone with God. This is part of the process of "abiding in Christ." Jesus used the metaphor of a vine and branches to describe our dependent relationship with the Father:

> Remain in Me, and I in you. Just as a branch is unable to produce fruit by itself unless it remains on the vine, so neither can you unless you remain in Me.
>
> "I am the vine; you are the branches. The one who remains in Me and I in him produces much fruit, because you can do nothing without Me.
> John 15:4-5 (HCSB)

When we abide (or remain) with Jesus through a healthy and regular devotional life, we are far better equipped to abide in Him as we go about our daily work and service to others.

He will produce fruit that not only sustains us but also feeds the world around us that is hungry for something that really satisfies.

Spending time in the secret place should never be about legalism, for it's all about getting better acquainted and growing deeper in love with the Person of Jesus Christ. It's where we rest in the comfort of Abba's arms and listen as He teaches us what brings Him joy and what brings Him sorrow. It's where we learn to live a life led by the Spirit.

In most of the world's religions, union with god is accomplished through arduous practice, lifelong rule-keeping, and aimless inward searches. No one ever seems to make it there, and the people who supposedly did are either dead or inaccessible. But one of the most beautiful hallmarks of Christianity is that we have a wide open invitation to union with our Father, paid for by the Son. We have no mountain to climb, because Jesus already climbed it for us. God is always waiting for us in the secret place with arms stretched wide.

8 IN THOUGHT

There is a written confessional prayer that millions of Christians around the world recite before partaking in the Lord's Supper:

"Most merciful God, we confess that we have sinned against you in thought, word, and deed, by what we have done, and by what we have left undone. We have not loved you with our whole heart; we have not loved our neighbors as ourselves. We are truly sorry and we humbly repent. For the sake of your Son Jesus Christ, have mercy on us and forgive us; that we may delight in your will, and walk in your ways, to the glory of your Name."[5]

This prayer eloquently and succinctly contains the essence of what this entire book is about. Let's reverse engineer it, however, and look at the content from the opposite vantage point: if we can sin against God in thought, word, and deed, it only follows that this is also how we worship Him. Satan, after all, has no creative ability. He can only hijack and corrupt what is meant to glorify God.

Most of us (certainly if you've made it this far reading this

---

[5] The Book Of Common Prayer, and Administration Of The Sacraments, and Other Rites and Ceremonies Of The Church. New York : New York Bible And Common Prayer Book Society, 1979.

book) are well acquainted with the concept of worshiping God with both words and actions. But what about your thoughts? Have you ever considered pouring out affection for Jesus with your mind? This is not a new idea. As a matter of fact, Jesus tells us that loving God with our whole self (heart, soul, and mind) is the greatest commandment:

> When the Pharisees heard that He had silenced the Sadducees, they came together. And one of them, an expert in the law, asked a question to test Him: "Teacher, which command in the law is the greatest?"
>
> He said to him, "Love the Lord your God with all your heart, with all your soul, and with all your mind. This is the greatest and most important command. The second is like it: Love your neighbor as yourself. All the Law and the Prophets depend on these two commands."
> Matthew 22:34-40 (HCSB)

In Luke 10:27, we also see the word "strength" added to the list: "heart, soul, mind, and strength." Jesus desires our total affection, not just one part. This leads us back to the original thesis of this book: that our lives are "living stones" that are the sanctuary for God's presence. The entirety of our being should be a "living sacrifice" to God, which Paul says is our "spiritual worship."

Have you ever heard the expression, "An idle mind is the Devil's playground"? It's true! When we fail to guard our thoughts, our minds become fertile soul for Satan to plant seeds of destruction. Pride, envy, lust, anger, gluttony, greed, laziness—this list that has become known as the "seven deadly sins"—all of them start in the mind. Sin doesn't usually start with with what is obviously "deadly," however. Usually, Satan begins with something benign...like boredom. You only need to look at some of the many millions of viral internet videos to realize that boredom makes people profoundly stupid! In my own life, I can attest that few things make me vulnerable to sin's temptation like boredom. Add to boredom apathy, entitlement, pride, offense, carelessness, and laziness. The enemy is a master at exploiting these seemingly minor offenses and turning them into the driving forces behind how we live.

Unfortunately, even within the Church, most of us have allowed our minds to be discipled by the world. We feed boredom with the internet, with movies, and with binge-watching shows on Netflix! I'm not saying that there's necessarily any evil in enjoying entertainment and technology, but it must be acknowledged that these things go a long way into shaping the way we think. If we continually feed our minds with how the world thinks, we inevitably conform the way we think as well. In the end, we can expect no other result than to exhibit the fruit of what we've been feeding ourselves.

Paul actually warns us about this *immediately* following the verse about being a "living sacrifice":

> Therefore, brothers, by the mercies of God, I urge you to present your bodies as a living sacrifice, holy and pleasing to God; this is your spiritual worship. Do not be conformed to this age, but be transformed by the renewing of your mind, so that you may discern what is the good, pleasing, and perfect will of God.
> Romans 12:1-2 (HCSB)

In other words, the very definition of a "living sacrifice" is a person who lives differently from the rest of the world, whose life is molded by the perfect will of God and not the prevailing wisdom, opinions, or culture of the age. And how do we go about living such a transformed life? By completely changing the way we think. This doesn't mean that we don't engage in culture, far from it. But it does mean that we aim toward a higher standard, for we have been called upward by Christ Himself (Philippians 3:14).

This process of renewal begins with humility, understanding that each of us in the Body of Christ has an important role to play. We serve each other by following the example of Jesus, who did not consider Himself too good for the task of washing his disciples' feet.

> For by the grace given to me, I tell everyone among you not to think of himself more highly than he should think. Instead, think sensibly, as God has distributed a measure of faith to each one. Now as we have many parts in one body, and all the parts do not have the same function, in the same way we who are many are one body in Christ and individually members of one another. According to the grace given to us, we have different gifts:
>
> If prophecy,
> use it according to the standard of one's faith;
> if service, in service;
> if teaching, in teaching;
> if exhorting, in exhortation;
> giving, with generosity;
> leading, with diligence;
> showing mercy, with cheerfulness.
> Romans 12:3-8 (HCSB)

The grace-given gifts that the Spirit bestows on us don't exist for us to think more highly of ourselves or as a means of self-promotion. They are for the building up of the Body, with each member being accountable to the others. The old mind's natural mode of operation is to cling and grapple for position and power like Jacob did in Genesis, but the renewed mind recognizes that the greatest accomplishment we can aspire to in the Kingdom is to serve those around us with humility and thanksgiving (Matthew 20:26).

Paul goes on in this chapter to list some of the foundational ethics that guide how the believer thinks differently than the world around him:

> Love must be without hypocrisy. Detest evil; cling to what is good. Show family affection to one another with brotherly love. Outdo one another in

> showing honor.
> Romans 12:9-10 (HCSB)

I love this part of the chapter because of how Paul seems to randomly throw "detest evil" into the middle of a paragraph about love. But it's not random at all. Paul says that, as Christians, our love is to be different than the love of the fallen world we live in. But how can we say that we love differently if we still cling to evil instead of good? How could we ever love the world in a way that brings life if we continue to give space in our lives to dead and broken things? Essentially, Paul is echoing what King David prayed in Psalm 86: "give me an undivided heart." Love that comes from a heart divided between righteousness and evil is hypocritical. Instead, we must *cling* to what is good, casting aside everything that leads us into the snares of temptation.

It's important to recognize that it's not enough to only detest evil; we have to cling to what's good as well. I know a lot of people who get bogged down in habitual sin and genuinely feel bad about it. They repent. They confess. They detest the evil so much that sometimes they forget who they are (God's chosen saints) and start defining themselves by their mistakes. Satan loves to leverage shame and turn it into self loathing, isolation, and hopelessness. It's not difficult to detest the evil, but often we forget to also cling to the good. Hitting the mark is nearly impossible if we don't look at the target. If we're going to live a life of radical love for Jesus and for the world that He loves, we must both detest the evil of our old flesh and *cling* to His goodness. Keep your eyes fixed on Jesus' gaze, allowing the finality of His work on the cross to be your unshakeable foundation. It's by the power of His Spirit that we are victorious over sin.

> Do not lack diligence; be fervent in spirit; serve the Lord. Rejoice in hope; be patient in affliction; be persistent in prayer.
> Romans 12:11-12 (HCSB)

Don't give up! Don't neglect to serve God, even when things get rough. Celebrate the promises of God over your life and be patient while He brings them to pass in His timing, always praying for God's will to be accomplished. Perseverance is part of the fruit of the Spirit, which means that it's something that doesn't come naturally but from spending time with God, allowing the Holy Spirit to renew our minds and strengthen our will to endure. Persevere with with a hopeful, optimistic outlook on the bright future that God has in store.

> Share with the saints in their needs; pursue hospitality. Bless those who persecute you; bless and do not curse.
> Romans 12:13-14 (HCSB)

Again, I love that Paul puts these two ideas back to back. He echoes what Jesus says in the Sermon on the Mount (Matthew 5:35). Be hospitable to the fellow saints, but don't stop there. Extend your hospitality to those who mock you and punish you for your faith. Jesus says we should pray for the people who persecute us, and that this is the character of the Father's children. It's easy to be a blessing to people who love you and treat you well, but it takes an entirely different mindset to bless those who bring you pain. Over the centuries, many multitudes have come to Christ because of the kindness of someone they persecuted.

Paul himself knew what it was like to be on the other end of this equation. The jarring image of Stephen's stoning must have been etched in his memory. Faced with persecution, Stephen's accusers (including Paul) saw a man whose "face was like the face of an angel" (Acts 6). Instead of cursing and condemning, in the face of death, Stephen looked up and saw a vision of Jesus Himself. With his dying breath, Stephen forgave Paul and all the others who were stoning him (Acts 7).

This is a radical love, a supernatural generosity we're talking about! It begins with cultivating generosity and kindness in our thoughts toward those who bring us pain, forgiving those who have wronged us without expecting an apology. Anyone can love a person who generously loves them back, but loving your enemies is profound and life-changing.

> Rejoice with those who rejoice; weep with those who weep.
> Romans 12:15 (HCSB)

Part of this radical love is to partake in Christ-like compassion for people we encounter, both friends and strangers. Frequently throughout the Gospels, before Jesus moved in healing or breakthrough power, He was moved by great compassion for those who came to Him. I believe that this Godly compassion is one of the biggest keys to experiencing God's breakthrough in times of trouble. We must not get discouraged by the tension between this world and the Kingdom we belong to. In God's eyes, there is no conflict between mourning with someone and having great faith for their breakthrough. Scripture calls us to do both.

Having great faith isn't about saying the right words or a pop-psychology phenomenon like "mind over matter." Great faith is capable of quietly trusting in the Lord, even while feeling the brunt of our dire circumstances. Often we try to shield ourselves from feeling somebody else's pain, as if we're doctors trying to maintain some sort of professional distance; but Jesus did nothing of the sort, instead taking on our pain as His own, bearing our sicknesses on the cross, taking the punishment of our bad decisions upon Himself. He has commissioned us to embrace hurting people and mourn with them. Simultaneously, He has given us the authority to bring the touch of Heaven into their circumstance. We have the knowledge, by faith, that on the last day, every single tear will be dried (Revelation 21:4); and so here, in these brief moments we have on earth, we know that not a single tear shed escapes God's notice (Psalm 56). Our Jesus is perfectly compassionate and perfectly powerful, and He calls us to carry that Gospel with us wherever we go.

Simultaneously, Paul issues the call for us to rejoice with people who are rejoicing. It seems so simple, so why is this even worth mentioning? Because some of Satan's most effective weapons are jealousy, bitterness, and entitlement.

Often, we preclude ourselves from God's blessings because we will not rejoice with someone who has received their breakthrough before we have. Instead of joining the Father's feast He set out for our brother, we complain that we deserve it more than they did. It's easy to miss, but one of the most powerful verses in the parable of the Prodigal Son is when the Father says to his eldest, "Son, you are always with me, and everything I have is yours" (Luke 15:31). All the riches of Heaven are already in our account as we are co-heirs with Christ, but when we refuse to rejoice with those who rejoice, we prove that we're not yet mature enough to have access to them.

> Be in agreement with one another. Do not be proud; instead, associate with the humble. Do not be wise in your own estimation.
> Romans 12:16 (HCSB)

Here's a big one we stumble over in the Church. My wife and I have the privilege of ministering across all manner of denominational streams. We often find ourselves in a Baptist church one day, an Anglican church the next, and a Pentecostal church the day after that. In each one, we are continually amazed at the powerful work that God is doing. No one has the market cornered on the Holy Spirit. Yet we frequently hear one movement using doctrinal excuses to dismiss how God is using the other. Instead of unifying and running together as one Body, we walk with a limp because we've severed off a foot over here and a hand over there. Some of the most viciously unbiblical statements I've ever heard inside the Church have come from one Christian leader slandering the other. How telling it is that Jesus' only recorded prayer for the Church is that we might be unified with God and unified with each other (John 17). Christ says that our unity (which is not the same thing as uniformity, mind you) will be one of the markers by which the world recognizes that the Gospel is true.

This, of course, doesn't dismiss us from studying the Word and holding fast to Scriptural orthodoxy and core doctrinal truths, especially those found in our common creeds like the

Apostles Creed and the Nicene Creed. However, our church disagreements are most often a greater reflection of our own insecurity than they are any kind of honest assessment of another person or ministry's standing with God. Paul elaborates on this subject in his letter to the Philippians. He writes that even when the Gospel is preached out of false motives, he still finds reason to rejoice:

> To be sure, some preach Christ out of envy and strife, but others out of good will. These do so out of love, knowing that I am appointed for the defense of the gospel; the others proclaim Christ out of rivalry, not sincerely, seeking to cause me anxiety in my imprisonment. What does it matter? Just that in every way, whether out of false motives or true, Christ is proclaimed. And in this I rejoice.
> Philippians 1:16-18 (HCSB)

I could probably write an entire book on this subject, and perhaps one day I will. For now, my fervent prayer is that as we actively participate in the renewal of our minds, we will allow the Holy Spirit to convict us when we're tempted to wield doctrine as a weapon against fellow believers rather than pray for them with thanksgiving for what God is doing in and through them. As for me, like Paul, I will rejoice whenever Christ is proclaimed and do what I can to serve the whole Church to the best of my ability.

> Do not repay anyone evil for evil. Try to do what is honorable in everyone's eyes. If possible, on your part, live at peace with everyone. Friends, do not avenge yourselves; instead, leave room for His wrath. For it is written: Vengeance belongs to Me; I will repay, says the Lord.
>
> But if your enemy is hungry, feed him. If he is thirsty, give him something to drink. For in so doing you will be heaping fiery coals on his head. Do not be conquered by evil, but conquer evil

> with good.
> Romans 12:17-21 (HCSB)

"Conquer evil with good." This is the essence of what we're called to in the Kingdom of God, the very thing that Christ accomplished on the cross that He has now called us to co-labor in. We must remember that our true enemy is not any man or woman here on earth, but the powers of darkness (Ephesians 6:12).

Conquering evil with good begins with knowing what is good in the first place, and that is why we renew our minds: so that we might carry out the will of God. Our two greatest assets in this process are the Holy Spirit, who dwells within us and teaches us (John 14:26) and the written Word of God; and these two always work in harmony with one another. The renewed mind forms its thoughts based on the Word and the voice of the Spirit. As we discussed before, the Holy Spirit illuminates what we read in Scripture, and it is essential to know the Scripture in order to consistently and accurately discern the Spirit's voice. In addition, being submitted to authority and involvement in a local church is vital for long-term spiritual growth, for the discernment of God's voice, and for the renewal of our minds. A lone sheep does not survive long on its own without the safety of the flock and the protective guidance of a shepherd. We grow in faith together as one Body, unified in our pursuit of Christ and His Kingdom.

This reformation of our thoughts takes commitment and faithful practice, and we can look to the example of the Nazirites for inspiration. Where they consecrated their physical food and drink, we consecrate what we feed our hearts. Where they consecrated the hair of their heads, we consecrate our thoughts to the glory of God. Where they consecrated their bodies against things that were dead, we consecrate our spiritual bodies against that which kills the soul, instead surrounding ourselves with that which brings life.

As we just did with Romans 12, we must continue studying

the Word for insight into God's will. There are a few major, foundational things that we can know for certain are the will of God, and meditating on these is an act of worship in and of itself that pleases God (Psalm 19:14).

Perhaps one of the most important aspects of God's will that should utterly transform how we think is that He desires that every person be saved.

> First of all, then, I urge that petitions, prayers, intercessions, and thanksgivings be made for everyone, for kings and all those who are in authority, so that we may lead a tranquil and quiet life in all godliness and dignity. This is good, and it pleases God our Savior, who wants everyone to be saved and to come to the knowledge of the truth.
> I Timothy 2:1-4

I'm not talking about universalism (the belief that all will go to Heaven regardless whether they put their faith in Christ), and neither was the Apostle Paul. However, Jesus died for all, and knowing this should influence every interaction we have with other people, especially those outside the Christian faith. It's easy to slip into an "us vs. them" mentality, regarding certain people with certain kinds of problems as untouchable, but Jesus demonstrated with His life that even the ones the world (or the religious community) regards as untouchable can find healing through His touch. He has commissioned us as His disciples to co-labor in His healing work, preaching the Gospel to the entire world (Mark 16:15) through both our actions and words. This is not just the work of ordained clergy, full-time church staff, or a special class of Christian. It is the call of every follower of Jesus.

For that reason, we must do as Paul says to Timothy, and pray for everyone—people of both high and low position—that they would come to know the Lord and submit to His will for their life to be saved. Notice that Paul doesn't say to pray *against* people but that we should pray *for* them with thanksgiving. Again, this stretches us beyond what our old process of thinking would allow. This might even lead us to pray for ourselves, that God would grant us His grace and affection for others so that we might be genuinely thankful for them.

Think about that for a moment: who in your life do you find it difficult to be thankful for? Take a moment and ask the Lord to help you change your heart for them, that He would teach you to see them as He sees them. Then, pray for them with gratitude that God created them, that He loves them, and that He has a purpose for them. Give thanks for the political leaders on the opposite side of your political views. Give thanks for people who don't like you. Give thanks for people who have hurt you. Pray for God to bless them, that through His extreme kindness, they would repent (Romans 2:4) and come to know Him.

This is radical stuff, isn't it? This mindset doesn't come all at once, and our flesh fiercely resists it. But I believe the Spirit of God searches for those who are willing to surrender their own desires in place of His will, and He will rest His presence and favor on their lives. And where the Spirit of the Lord is, there is true liberty (2 Corinthians 3:17). Let us pursue with determination the will of God in this way, so that we may carry with us the revolutionary love that empowered Paul and Silas to lead their prison warden to Christ after they were beaten and chained (Acts 16). They could have let the man who oversaw their torture commit suicide, but instead they saved his life and preached the Gospel to him and his family.

> "Now if the wicked person turns from all the sins he has committed, keeps all My statutes, and does what is just and right, he will certainly live; he will not die. None of the transgressions he has committed will be held against him. He will live because of the righteousness he has practiced. Do I take any pleasure in the death of the wicked?" This is the declaration of the Lord God. "Instead, don't I take pleasure when he turns from his ways and lives?
> Ezekiel 18:21 (HCSB)

God desires that all would turn from wickedness and

follow Him in lives of righteousness. The prophet Ezekiel goes on to say again in verse 32 that God takes no pleasure in anyone's death, that He desires that all will live! This is the Gospel for both the Church and the world that does not yet know Him. **This call to righteousness is yet another aspect of the Lord's will that we can know for certain, and we should let that truth sink deep into our bones.**

True righteousness isn't about rule keeping, and the Old Testament demonstrates to us that following righteousness as a legal construct simply isn't enough. In order to live righteously before God, we must be covered by the righteousness of Christ. This can only be accomplished by faith. If this weren't the case, the Pharisees would truly have been closer to God than anyone else, but Jesus saw right through their faithless rule keeping.

The principle of righteousness by faith has always been the the truth, as Paul teaches us in Romans 4. He points to Abraham (who was first called Abram), whom God chose as the patriarch of His people:

> Abram believed the Lord, and He credited it to him as righteousness.
> Genesis 15:6 (HCSB)

King David also had this revelation of God's incredible mercy, and he expressed his faith through worship:

> How joyful is the one
> whose transgression is forgiven,
> whose sin is covered!
> How joyful is the man
> the Lord does not charge with sin
> and in whose spirit is no deceit!
> Psalm 32:1-2 (HCSB)

Faith in Jesus is what empowers us to live righteous lives. It's not just that Jesus' righteousness hides our sin from sight but that He put it to death on the cross. Now, we join Him daily, taking up our cross and putting to death the old self:

> Therefore, put to death what belongs to your worldly nature: sexual immorality, impurity, lust, evil desire, and greed, which is idolatry. Because of these, God's wrath comes on the disobedient, and you once walked in these things when you were living in them. But now you must also put away all the following: anger, wrath, malice, slander, and filthy language from your mouth. Do not lie to one another, since you have put off the old self with its practices and have put on the new self. You are being renewed in knowledge according to the image of your Creator.
> Colossians 3:5-10 (HCSB)

Again, Jesus reversed the old way of thinking: we don't strive for righteous living in order to obtain salvation for ourselves. Righteousness isn't the finish line! Instead, our starting point is the righteousness of Christ which has been credited to us because we have faith in Him. Because of this beautiful exchange, we are now empowered to live righteous lives, free of shame and the sin that causes it. We actively renew our minds so that the thoughts of the old self will give way to the thoughts of God, that His will would be manifest in our lives.

The Apostle John, whose identity was so rooted in Christ that he referred to himself as "the disciple Jesus loved," tells us that when we see Jesus as He really is, we will become like Him (1 John 3:2). The goal of transforming how we think is to see Jesus every day more clearly as He truly is so that we are empowered to live more and more like Him.

There are practical steps we can take to actively renew our minds, and I would like to take the rest of this chapter to lay out a few simple ways to begin. Quite simply, I believe this process is all about saturating our thoughts with the Word and the Spirit. Psalm 1 sets up the entire book of Psalms—it is the thesis statement for all the others—and tells us what it's really all about:

> How happy is the man
> who does not follow the advice of the wicked
> or take the path of sinners
> or join a group of mockers!
> Instead, his delight is in the Lord's instruction,
> and he meditates on it day and night.
> He is like a tree planted beside streams of water
> that bears its fruit in season
> and whose leaf does not wither.
> Whatever he does prospers.
> Psalm 1:1-3 (HCSB)

Meditating on the Lord's instructions day and night has a transformative effect on every aspect of life. This is unlike the mediation of Eastern religions, in which the participant empties his mind of all thought. Instead, when we mediate as Christians, we fill our thoughts up with the majesty of God and His Word. Paul echoes the Psalmist in his letter to the Philippians:

> Finally brothers, whatever is true, whatever is honorable, whatever is just, whatever is pure, whatever is lovely, whatever is commendable — if there is any moral excellence and if there is any praise — dwell on these things.
> Philippians 4:8 (HCSB)

There was a monk named Brother Lawrence at the Carmelite monastery in Paris in the 1600s who referred to this day and night mediation on God as "practicing the presence of God." He made it his life-long exercise to think constantly on the love of Jesus, worshiping Him with his thoughts throughout his daily work, his recreation, as well as the appointed times of prayer and worship with his brothers at the monastery. Here is how Brother Lawrence described this practice in a letter to a close friend:

> *I worshipped Him the oftenest I could, keeping my mind in*

> *His holy presence and recalling it as often as I found it wandered from Him. I made this my business, not only at the appointed times of prayer but all the time; every hour, every minute, even in the height of my work, I drove from my mind everything that interrupted my thoughts of God.*
>
> *I found no small pain in this exercise. Yet I continued it, notwithstanding all the difficulties that occurred. And I tried not to trouble or disquiet myself when my mind wandered. Such has been my common practice ever since I entered religious life. Though I have done it very imperfectly, I have found great advantages by it. These, I well know, are to be imputed to the mercy and goodness of God because we can do nothing without Him; and I still less than any.*
>
> *When we are faithful to keep ourselves in His holy presence, and set Him always before us, this hinders our offending Him and doing anything that may displease Him. It also begets in us a holy freedom, and, if I may so speak, a familiarity with God, where, when we ask, He supplies the graces we need. Over time, by often repeating these acts, they become habitual, and the presence of God becomes quite natural to us.*[6]

One of my favorite things about Brother Lawrence's process is that he didn't allow himself to be discouraged when he failed. He simply thanked God for His grace and returned his thoughts to Him as swiftly as possible. It is a simple, beautiful model to follow.

One of my own habits is to mediate on particular passages of Scripture, especially ones that speak to our purpose here on earth or on the nature of Jesus, praying it until it becomes a natural part of my thought process. I frequently return to the fruit of the Spirit, reminding myself that because the Holy Spirit lives inside me, these character attributes are now my own nature. Often I'll go through the list while I'm out for a run, driving in my car, or doing some simple menial task like

---

[6] "First Letter." Lawrence, and John J. Delaney. 1977. The practice of the presence of God. Public Domain.

washing dishes. Written out, my thought process might look a bit like this:

The fruit of the Spirit is…

- **Love** - Because the Spirit has taken up residence within me, love is my natural state of being. It permeates all that I do because it permeates all that God is. I will live out of His nature of Love, extending it to every person I come into contact with. He loves me; therefore I love Him and everything He loves.
- **Joy** - Because the Holy Spirit lives in me, joyfulness saturates my personality. In every situation, whether in celebration or grieving, I will be joyful. Even when I don't *feel* joy in my emotions, I will actively rejoice in God's goodness. In His joy, I find my strength to face any situation.
- **Peace** - Because I have the Comforter making His home inside of me, I am peaceful at all times. Turmoil and confusion are no longer drivers of my decisions. This peace is more than than an emotion, it is a Person in whose arms I have supernatural rest at all times.
- **Patience** - Because the Holy Spirit works in me and through me, I am patient with every thing and every person. I have been gifted with strength and endurance to run a good race, enduring every trial with the same strength that raised Jesus from the dead.
- **Kindness** - Because the Holy Spirit lives within me, His kindness flows through me in all my actions. To every person I meet, I will give the same kindness that Christ has shown to me.
- **Goodness** - Because my body is the temple of the Holy Spirit, God's goodness and mercy chase after me every day of my life. God is perfectly good, and there is no evil in Him. Because I no longer live, but Christ lives in me, His goodness saturates every fiber of my being and gives me the courage and strength to live a righteous life.
- **Faith** - Because the Holy Spirit has made His home in me, I am a person of great faith. My expectations are not based on what I have or have not experienced but on the miraculous standard of God's Word. My prayers carry

power because faith has been credited to me as righteousness. I will not timidly dismiss or make excuses for the impossible things I am called to do in the Bible but joyfully approach every situation knowing that with God all things are possible.
- **Gentleness** - Because the Holy Spirit is my constant Companion, every word I speak and every action I take are measured in gentleness. I will, like Christ, lay down my life like a lamb to the slaughter. When I am tempted to react to others in harshness (whether or not I am right or wrong), I will hold my tongue and intercede for them instead.
- **Self-control** - Because the Spirit of Christ is in me, I will walk daily in the completed work of the Cross. Temptation will not rule over me because sin has already been defeated.

It goes without saying that I frequently fall short of the high standards set in this list. But, like Brother Lawrence, I am learning not to be discouraged when I don't live up to the new identity God has given to me. Instead, I dust myself off, repent to God, and continue walking in gratitude of His amazing grace. What I can tell you is that meditating on these truths from God's Word often stops me in my tracks. In moments where I find myself getting impatient with a customer service agent on the phone, I feel the Holy Spirit remind me that I am patient and kind. In moments when when I feel like giving up on the calling God placed on my life because there seems to be little progress, I feel the Spirit breathe faith into my soul for things not yet seen. When I'm tempted to lash out because somebody has hurt me, I feel the Spirit nudge me, reminding me that I have the gentleness of Christ Himself guiding my words and actions. Making a habit of pondering the Word, allowing the Holy Spirit access to convict and change our behavior, has an undeniable impact on daily living.

You can phrase your meditations any way you like, in your own words, as a declaration or as a request to God. What matters is not how eloquent you are but that the Truth of the Gospel consumes your thoughts, even as you go about your day-to-day chores. You can form this practice with all manner of Scripture: the great narrative stories of Genesis, the Beatitudes, the words of Jesus on the cross, etc..

A close friend of mine spent a long season of her life meditating on the image of Jesus in John's Revelation:

> I turned to see whose voice it was that spoke to me. When I turned I saw seven gold lampstands, and among the lampstands was One like the Son of Man, dressed in a long robe and with a gold sash wrapped around His chest. His head and hair were white like wool — white as snow — and His eyes like a fiery flame. His feet were like fine bronze as it is fired in a furnace, and His voice like the sound of cascading waters. He had seven stars in His right hand; a sharp double-edged sword came from His mouth, and His face was shining like the sun at midday.
> Revelation 1:12-16 (HCSB)

My friend read this passage over and over again until she had it memorized, pondering it throughout her day. She recently told me that sometimes, when she prays for another person in need, this is the image of Jesus she sees in her mind, and seeing it causes great faith to spring up inside of her!

This kind of meditation on Scripture that Christ Church Nashville has done every Sunday with Psalm 95 for several years now. At first, I asked myself, "Why do they repeat this same Psalm every Sunday? Can't they move on to something else?" But then, slowly, it began to sink in: "For the Lord is a great God, a great King above all Gods." What I used to glance over now shakes me to the core every time I read it, and I can hardly speak those words out loud any longer without being moved to tears. Even now, as I write them, I feel that familiar lump forming in my throat and my eyes welling up. He is indeed a great God!

We sometimes read the language of Scripture and repeat it

in Church culture so often that we miss what it actually means. It can be easy, even habitual, to sing familiar songs in our worship gatherings without actually pondering what it is we're saying. Doing so can cause our songs to become lifeless and our time in God's presence to feel empty, leaving us wondering where God is in the midst of our every day lives. Instead of worshiping God passionately, our flesh tempts us to go through the motions, lose faith, or not worship at all.

God created our emotions to serve Him, but when God's proper order gets reversed, our emotions can become awful tyrants. God created us to feel, and He speaks to us through intangible moments and thoughts. However, it is vital that these tools fall under God's sovereignty and the authority of the Bible. Part of worshiping God with our minds is drawing our souls (mind, will, and emotions) into alignment with God's will.

King David knew this challenge, and in Psalm 103, he sets a marvelous example of how to bring our emotions back under the authority of God's truth (rather than the perceived truth of our feelings which are not always honest):

> My soul, praise Yahweh,
> and all that is within me, praise His holy name.
> My soul, praise the Lord,
> and do not forget all His benefits.
> He forgives all your sin;
> He heals all your diseases.
> He redeems your life from the Pit;
> He crowns you with faithful love and compassion.
> He satisfies you with goodness;
> your youth is renewed like the eagle.
> Psalm 103:1-5 (HCSB)

The the King James Version translates verse 1, "Bless the Lord, oh my soul. And all that is within me bless His holy name." Here David is commanding his own soul to worship God, calling his mind, will, and emotions to fulfill their created purpose. I'm not always going to *feel* like worshiping God with all that is in me, but in those moments, I can follow

David's example and command my soul to do so.

How David arrives there is just as important. He does it by reminding himself of God's faithfulness. There's an interesting passage in Revelation in which John falls down to worship an angel that was giving him the tour of Heaven, but the angel stops him and redirects him to worship Jesus:

> Then I fell at his feet to worship him, but he said to me, "Don't do that! I am a fellow slave with you and your brothers who have the testimony about Jesus. **Worship God, because the testimony about Jesus is the spirit of prophecy."**
> Revelation 19:10

What the angel says to John here in this moment is incredibly powerful and full of Heavenly insight. There are moments, even times full of good intentions, when our focus drifts away from Jesus, and we are tempted to worship what is intended to bring Him glory instead of worshiping Jesus Himself. But the angel's words echo David's in Psalm 103: "forget not His benefits." The angel says, "The testimony about Jesus is the spirit of prophecy." In other words, our testimonies, our stories about what Jesus has done, are actually prophetic in nature. By recalling what God has done in the past, we are reminded of what kinds of things God is interested in and what He is willing to do again. He forgives sin. He heals every kind of disease. He redeems the most lost and hopeless life. He pours out perfect love and compassion. He satisfies from His endless goodness and gives strength to rise above every circumstance.

Recalling God's goodness and faithfulness gives us courage to face any situation and redirects our souls back to worship the only One who is worthy of worship. I believe it is vital for spiritual health to stay encouraged by keeping testimonies before our eyes. Don't forget His benefits! Take every opportunity to rejoice in what God has done for you and for the people around you. If you hear a testimony of God providing for someone else the very thing you've been asking

Him for, don't be discouraged! Instead worship Jesus and thank Him for allowing you to hear a prophetic testimony of His goodness.

In every circumstance, worship God with all your mind, will, and emotions. Don't forget how good He is or the things He has done. Meditate on His Word. Allow the Truth in Scripture and the Holy Spirit's instruction to completely reshape the way you think so that your life will be transformed into the likeness of Jesus.

As we treasure God's Word and the Spirit's voice, the thoughts of the flesh are put to death and replaced with the thoughts of God. As we worship the Lord with our minds, God begins to reveal the deep mysteries of His nature to us so that we might become more like Him. Mere human intellect is surpassed and supplanted by the wisdom and knowledge of the Holy Spirit.

> But as it is written:
> What eye did not see and ear did not hear,
> and what never entered the human mind —
> God prepared this for those who love Him.
> Now God has revealed these things to us by the Spirit, for the Spirit searches everything, even the depths of God. For who among men knows the thoughts of a man except the spirit of the man that is in him? In the same way, no one knows the thoughts of God except the Spirit of God. Now we have not received the spirit of the world, but the Spirit who comes from God, so that we may understand what has been freely given to us by God. We also speak these things, not in words taught by human wisdom, but in those taught by the Spirit, explaining spiritual things to spiritual people.
> I Corinthians 2:7-13 (HCSB)

As we surrender our minds as a sanctuary for the Holy Spirit, God has already prepared knowledge and wisdom for us that could have never been known apart from Him.

Human wisdom and intellect are amazing gifts but, by themselves, aren't enough to know God. What God asks of us isn't that we have a high IQ but a surrendered heart. We see in the book of Acts that God used Peter, an uneducated fisherman, to confound the intellectuals of his day because the Spirit living within him transformed his mind. Let it be so of us as well, daily resolving to worship God with all our mind.

9 IN WORD

If you polled military experts, I think you would probably find universal agreement that this was the worst battle strategy in the history of mankind...

Faced with the impending invasion of three enemy nations who had joined forces to destroy the kingdom of Judah, King Jehoshaphat chose a tactic that defied all logic. Instead of seeking military help from nearby kingdoms, He placed the survival of his kingdom in the hands of God himself. Rather than sending out chariots or his most battle-tested warriors to fight on the front lines., he selected a group of singers and worshipers to march ahead of the army and shout praises to God! As a musician, I can tell you this much from personal experience: musicians aren't usually the ones who you should entrust with matters of national security. I can't even imagine what it must have felt like to be in that worship team!

King Jehoshaphat was a reformer. In a long line of mostly bad kings throughout Judah's history, Jehoshaphat was one of a few good ones, and though his reign wasn't perfect, the Bible tells us that God was with him because he followed in the righteous path of his great-great-great-grandfather King David. God blessed Jehoshaphat and the kingdom of Judah in all manner of ways. The kingdom's education system was thriving. Their military might was on the rise. The economy grew in tremendous wealth, as even neighboring rivals such as the Philistines and the Arabs brought bountiful gifts and tributes into the kingdom. All of this, however, also made Judah a big target for foreign invaders.

At first, King Jehoshaphat applied what seemed like a sensible strategy to ensure national security. He formed an alliance with his neighbors in Israel (Judah and the rest of the Israelite kingdom were divided in two at this point), but King Ahab of Israel was an evil man who hated God's prophets. Jehoshaphat's strategy failed spectacularly in a battle that resulted in Ahab's violent death. After the battle, the prophet Jehu sharply reprimanded King Jehoshaphat for making an alliance with wicked leaders, and Jehoshaphat responded by making sure that, moving forward, all of Judah was overseen by righteous judges and instructed by the Levites in God's Law.

The foreign threats persisted, this time bigger than ever. The Moabites, Ammonites, and Meunites banded together with the intent to destroy Judah once and for all. Having learned his lesson, Jehoshaphat did not look outward to seek help from political or military allies. Instead, he proclaimed a fast for the entire kingdom and gathered them together, seeking the Lord for deliverance from the enemy. A vast assembly from every city in Judah gathered at the courtyard of the temple in Jerusalem. There, in the presence of his entire kingdom, Jehoshaphat offered up a desperate prayer to God:

> Yahweh, the God of our ancestors, are You not the God who is in Heaven, and do You not rule over all the kingdoms of the nations? Power and might are in Your hand, and no one can stand against You. Are You not our God who drove out the inhabitants of this land before Your people Israel and who gave it forever to the descendants of Abraham Your friend? They have lived in the land and have built You a sanctuary in it for Your name and have said, "If disaster comes on us — sword or judgment, pestilence or famine — we will stand before this

> temple and before You, for Your name is in this temple. We will cry out to You because of our distress, and You will hear and deliver."
>
> Now here are the Ammonites, Moabites, and the inhabitants of Mount Seir. You did not let Israel invade them when Israel came out of the land of Egypt, but Israel turned away from them and did not destroy them. Look how they repay us by coming to drive us out of Your possession that You gave us as an inheritance. Our God, will You not judge them? For we are powerless before this vast number that comes to fight against us. We do not know what to do, but we look to You.
>
> 2 Chronicles 20:6-12 (HCSB)

Just like we saw King David do in the last chapter with Psalm 103, Jehoshaphat stirred his heart to faith in God's rescue by recalling what God had already done. He placed all his hopes in the Lord, regardless whether he succeeded or failed, and somewhere in the midst of all the dire threats, recounting the testimonies of God's goodness gave him faith that God would bring deliverance.

God's response to Jehoshaphat's faith is spectacular! Suddenly, the Holy Spirit came upon Jahaziel, a Levite and one of the prophets, and he decreed instructions from God to the people of Judah:

> This is what the Lord says: 'Do not be afraid or discouraged because of this vast number, for the battle is not yours, but God's. Tomorrow, go down against them. You will see them coming up the Ascent of Ziz, and you will find them at the end of the valley facing the Wilderness of Jeruel. **You do not have to fight this battle. Position yourselves, stand still, and see the salvation of the Lord. He is with you, Judah and Jerusalem. Do not be afraid or**

discouraged. Tomorrow, go out to face them, for Yahweh is with you.'"

> Then Jehoshaphat bowed with his face to the ground, and all Judah and the inhabitants of Jerusalem fell down before the Lord to worship Him. Then the Levites from the sons of the Kohathites and the Korahites stood up to praise the Lord God of Israel shouting with a loud voice.
> 2 Chronicles 20:13-19 (HCSB)

The next day, King Jehoshaphat led the Judeans into the wilderness and implored them to trust in God and in His Word delivered by the prophets.

> Then he consulted with the people and appointed some to sing for the Lord and some to praise the splendor of His holiness. When they went out in front of the armed forces, they kept singing:
>
> Give thanks to the Lord,
> for His faithful love endures forever.
>
> The moment they began their shouts and praises, the Lord set an ambush against the Ammonites, Moabites, and the inhabitants of Mount Seir who came to fight against Judah, and they were defeated. The Ammonites and Moabites turned against the inhabitants of Mount Seir and completely annihilated them. When they had finished with the inhabitants of Seir, they helped destroy each other.
> 2 Chronicles 20:21-23 (HCSB)

The Apostle Paul reminds us in Ephesians 6 that today, our real enemies aren't foreign invading armies or any other people but the demonic powers of Satan and his armies of darkness. Ultimately, however, God's word to Jehoshaphat still applies: our battles belong to God. Without Him, we don't stand a chance, but with Him, we already have total victory.

Worship isn't just a nice thing we do at church. Our praise is an offensive weapon against the kingdom of darkness! The Bible is full of examples in which God's people chose to lift up their voices and praise the Lord in the face of impossible odds, and God moved upon their praise and brought breakthrough. It happened to Paul and Silas in prison: beaten and chained, they sang out Psalms of worship to the Lord, and the Holy Spirit moved in such power that the prison doors flew open and their chains fell off. It's what happened when Joshua led the armies of Israel around the city of Jericho: upon the shouts of His people, God shook the walls of the city down and gave them the victory. All throughout the Psalms, we see King David and the other writers praising God *before* they obtained breakthrough in their situations.

This is why it's vital to follow David's example in Psalm 103 and command our souls to "bless the Lord with all that is within," regardless of circumstance. As we discussed in Chapter 5, there is sometimes the temptation to sit back on our heels and let others do the worshiping when we don't feel like it; but all throughout the Bible, we find that worship isn't just a suggestion, it's a commandment. The book of Psalms closes with perhaps the most impassioned command to worship the Lord in all of Scripture:

> Hallelujah!
> Praise God in His sanctuary.
> Praise Him in His mighty Heavens.
> Praise Him for His powerful acts;
> praise Him for His abundant greatness.
> Praise Him with trumpet blast;
> praise Him with harp and lyre.
> Praise Him with tambourine and dance;
> praise Him with flute and strings.
> Praise Him with resounding cymbals;
> praise Him with clashing cymbals.
> Let everything that breathes praise the Lord.
> Hallelujah!
> Psalm 150 (HCSB)

The Hebrew word that gets translated "praise" in Psalm 150 is "halal," from which we get our word "hallelujah." It literally means to rave or give foolish, clamorous praise to God![7] It conjures up the image of David shedding his clothes and dancing wildly before the Ark of the Covenant as God's presence made its entrance into Jerusalem. There is tremendous power in lifting up the name of Jesus and worshiping him with our voices.

It goes without saying that clamorous praise may come more naturally to some people than it does to others. God designed each person's personality to be a unique reflection of His own character. Perhaps you are, by nature, a more quiet and reserved person. That's okay to a point, but God still deserves your most exuberant worship, regardless whether you are an introvert or an extrovert. I recently heard a pastor say that claiming it's not your personality to worship God passionately is essentially the same reasoning as claiming that your personality isn't well suited for righteousness. That statement stings, but it's true! Worshiping God and living righteously are both commandments, not suggestions.

When we set aside our circumstances and order our emotions to praise the Lord for who He is and what He has done, we position ourselves, like King Jehoshaphat, to see God win the day on our behalf. This is not a victory of striving but of surrender! Before the answer even materialized, Jehoshaphat began to recount God's goodness and extol His worthiness: "Power and might are in Your hand, and no one can stand against you!" There is something about worship that causes faith to rise, and we see throughout Scripture that faith moves the heart of God.

Singing or speaking aloud praises reminds us of our identity in Christ and His sovereignty over our situations. It compels our hearts into submission to His will and authority. When we give testimony to the things He has done through

---

[7] "Halal." Strong, James. 1890. *Strong's Exhaustive Concordance of the Bible*. Abingdon Press.

stories and songs, it recalls to our memory the perfect goodness, love, and power at the core of God's nature.

Most of us have heard the hymn "Turn Your Eyes Upon Jesus." I love the lyric Hellen Lemmel penned in 1922, originally titled "The Heavenly Vision": "and the things of earth will grow strangely dim in the light of His glory and grace." It's true! One of the chief goals of our worship is to fix our gaze clearly on Jesus, allowing the reality of Heaven to crowd out this earthly kingdom that is rapidly passing away.

Singing worship songs aloud to God is a bit like pledging allegiance to your country's flag or singing your national anthem, only we are now citizens of a Kingdom not of this world but of eternity in Christ. There are certain times that we sing our national anthem when the lyrics seem at odds with the political climate happening around us, but somewhere in the singing, we remind ourselves that we are loyal to higher ideals. In the United States, our national anthem concludes with the question, "Oh, say, does that Star Spangled Banner yet wave o'er the land of the free and the home of the brave?" That question is intended to make us ponder, are we still the land of the free and the home of the brave? Is there something I must do to ensure that this high ideal is a reality my children and grandchildren will still enjoy? So it is with our worship as well.

When we sing "and the things of this world will grow strangely dim," often those things are not dim at all. Sometimes, they are glaring, and the light of Jesus' glory and grace seem barely visible in the midst of our circumstances. But the hymn sets our hearts toward a higher mark than present circumstances, reminding us that there is much more to reality than what we see with our eyes. The Apostle Paul tells us in Romans 4 that we serve a God who "calls things into existence that do not exist." As we sing about the glory of God, even when our eyes do not perceive it, we come into agreement with Heaven's call to things that don't yet exist. Our battles belong to God, and He has already won the victory. When we praise God aloud, we shout "Amen!" to the promises of God, knowing that they are already delivered in

Christ, and God is glorified in fulfilling every one of them (2 Corinthians 1:20).

Sometimes we sing *because* we know it's true! Other times we sing *until* we know it's true! We see this pattern scattered throughout the Psalms as King David and the other writers acknowledge their hardships but never stop proclaiming the greatness of God. Some have pointed an accusing finger at modern worship songs, calling them disingenuous for not verbalizing the same kind of pain and sorrow we see in the Psalms. There may be some validity to that. However, on this side of the cross, even in the middle of terrible sorrow, I would much rather hold on to the victory of the cross than wallow in the agony of this fallen world.

There's nothing wrong with an honest acknowledgement of present pain and suffering to Jesus. Psalm 55 implores us to cast our cares on God. Jesus Himself offered up His agony to the Father in the garden of Gethsemane and on the cross. But Jesus' eyes weren't fixed on the cross itself, they were aimed beyond it, beyond the tomb, toward what was to come:

> Let us run with endurance the race that lies before us, keeping our eyes on Jesus, the source and perfecter of our faith, who for the joy that lay before Him endured a cross and despised the shame and has sat down at the right hand of God's throne.
> Hebrews 12:1b-2 (HCSB)

Jesus' sights were set on the joy beyond the cross, and now we, in turn, keep our eyes on Him! The things of the earth *will* grow strangely dim, and until they do, I will keep on singing!

There is actually a grave danger in neglecting our worship and failing to acknowledge God with our words. Just as worshiping Him with our words causes faith to rise, failing to do so causes faith to dwindle. There is a rather strange and alarming story in Luke's Gospel about what happened when Jesus ministered in his hometown of Nazareth. He entered the synagogue and was given the scroll of Isaiah to read. He read aloud what would have likely been a familiar Messianic prophecy to the people gathered there (a prophecy He knew pointed to Himself):

> The Spirit of the Lord is on Me,
> because He has anointed Me
> to preach good news to the poor.
> He has sent Me
> to proclaim freedom to the captives
> and recovery of sight to the blind,
> to set free the oppressed,
> to proclaim the year of the Lord's favor.
>
> He then rolled up the scroll, gave it back to the attendant, and sat down. And the eyes of everyone in the synagogue were fixed on Him. He began by saying to them, "Today as you listen, this Scripture has been fulfilled."
>
> They were all speaking well of Him and were amazed by the gracious words that came from His mouth, yet they said, "Isn't this Joseph's son?"
> Luke 4:18-22 (HCSB)

The verse there that says "they were speaking well of Him," often gets translated "they bore witness to Him." In other words, as Jesus read from the scroll, something inside the hearts of those gathered testified that His words were true. There was something about His reading that captivated their attention. Knowing what He had already done in the nearby town of Capernaum, His many healings and miracles, they were waiting for Jesus to *do something*.

But look what happened: they began to ask themselves, "Isn't this Joseph's son?" The crowd took their eyes off of who Jesus said He was (who He truly was) and instead fixed their gaze on what appeared to them in the natural. When I read this passage, it feels like the air is being let out of a balloon! All this hope, all this expectation vanishes the moment the people open their mouths and declare what seemed obvious (a "reality" that wasn't actually true). Whatever faith they had for that brief moment when they bore witness and spoke well of Him completely collapsed. *No, this can't be the Messiah. We know this kid. He's Joseph's son.* The Gospel of Mark's account of this story tells us that, because there was no faith, Jesus was unable to do many miracles and that Jesus was amazed at their unbelief. Look what happens next:

> Then He said to them, "No doubt you will quote this proverb to Me: 'Doctor, heal yourself. So all we've heard that took place in Capernaum, do here in Your hometown also.' "
>
> He also said, "I assure you: No prophet is accepted in his hometown. But I say to you, there were certainly many widows in Israel in Elijah's days, when the sky was shut up for three years and six months while a great famine came over all the land. Yet Elijah was not sent to any of them — but to a widow at Zarephath in Sidon. And in the prophet Elisha's time, there were many in Israel who had serious skin diseases, yet not one of them was healed — only Naaman the Syrian."
>
> When they heard this, everyone in the synagogue was enraged. They got up, drove Him out of town, and brought Him to the edge of the hill that their town was built on, intending to hurl Him over the cliff. But He passed right through the crowd and went on His way.
> Luke 4:23-30 (HCSB)

I find Jesus' examples from Elijah and Elisha's lives to be utterly fascinating. It must be noted that the goodness of God and His miraculous power remained unchanged, even when the nation of Israel had no regard for Him, and therefore, God looked outside of His own chosen people for opportunities to display His glory. By their lack of faith, the

Israelites forfeited their chance to experience God's power, and God instead found faith for the miraculous among foreigners. It wasn't His nature that had changed; it was the lack of faith in people who would not acknowledge Him.

These two accounts would have been a stinging rebuke to the religious community of Jesus' day. Surely *they*, gathered there at the synagogue on the Sabbath, were not the same kind of people who rejected the prophets. And surely Jesus could not have been the real Messiah if He couldn't see how much better they were than *those* people. But then they actually prove Jesus' point by trying to throw Him off a cliff!

Let's recap: the people of Nazareth had heard reports of Jesus working many miracles in Capernaum; they heard Him make a declaration of His identity; and something stirred inside of them that caused them, at first, to speak well of Him. However, they began questioning His credentials; and once He challenged their lack of faith, they tried to destroy Him. There's a lot to be learned here, but my big (and sobering) takeaway is this: **it's possible to have a face-to-face encounter with Jesus and leave completely unchanged if we fail to acknowledge Him for who He is.**

This principle follows if you continue to observe the Pharisees' interactions with Jesus. In Matthew 12, Jesus delivers a demon-possessed man, and immediately afterward, the Pharisees demand to see a "sign" from Him to prove His identity, as if casting out the demon weren't enough for them! When Jesus healed a lame man to prove He had authority to forgive the man's sins, the Pharisees walked away believing He had the right to do neither (Mark 2). When He healed the man with the shriveled arm, the Pharisees left to plot how they might kill Him (Mark 3). The final straw came when Jesus raised Lazarus from the dead (what bigger mark of authority could anyone have?), but the Pharisees responded by plotting to kill both Jesus and Lazarus to prevent anyone else from believing in Him. As they were hatching their plot, the high priest Caiaphas actually prophesied that Jesus' death would atone for all of God's people, yet still he joined the plot to crucify Jesus (John 11).

My point is that there is actually a marked danger in exposing ourselves to Jesus without responding to Him in the manner He deserves. The same as the Pharisees or the people of Nazareth, our hearts may become calloused, and our sins might metastasize like a cancer and consume our entire being. We might actually miss it when God moves; and, rather than worship Him for what He's doing, attempt to throw Him and His work off a cliff. How much more dangerous is it when we confess with our mouths that Jesus is the Messiah, the Son of the living God, yet we fail to respond to Him with wholehearted worship?

Ask yourself this question: how would you respond if Jesus walked into your Sunday church service, and you immediately recognized Him? Here is the Son of God standing in front of you! What would you do? Better yet, if you're a parent of small children, how might they respond to Him?

How does that response compare to the way you actually worship when you're at church? After all, we know that where two or three are gathered, He is there in our midst (Matthew 18). The Bible promises that God inhabits our praises (Psalm 22)! We have this amazing promise that God is with us when we gather together in unity and worship Him, but does our worship actually reflect that reality? If our response to the faith-filled knowledge that the Spirit of Christ is present doesn't look a lot like it would if Jesus entered the room in the flesh, something is off. Are we, like the Pharisees, always waiting for a bigger sign before we *really* give Jesus our worship, before we *really* commit to living with an undivided heart for Him? Each of us has heard the testimonies of other people who encountered the Lord, just like the Nazarenes heard from Capernaum. What's more, we have the Scripture and the Holy Spirit testifying within us. So, what are we waiting for?

Half-hearted worship causes faith to shrivel and die. Half-hearted worship caves to the pressures of the world and finds other objects of affection. Halfhearted worship rarely precedes breakthrough because it refuses to give thanksgiving in advance and often forgets to give thanks when God does move. I only say "rarely" because God's grace is too big for me to make a rule and say "never." As I have travelled and led many thousands of people in worship, I have seen a lot of powerful, passionate, whole-hearted praise; and I will gladly celebrate with anyone who celebrates the risen Jesus! But I've also seen a lot of weak-kneed, half-hearted worship; and I find that heartbreaking. Is God somehow less powerful when we don't worship Him? Certainly not! He remains unchanged for eternity, but that doesn't mean that we get to experience His benefits. It's *we* who miss out when we don't worship and praise. Not only that, the unsaved world suffers as well because our witness is rendered without power or sincerity.

Perhaps, as you're reading, you recognize that Jesus doesn't always get the praise from your lips that He deserves. Certainly, this is true of all of us at some point or other. Everyone has good days and bad days, but we don't have to stay there. The goal is to have fewer and fewer bad days, and more and more good days. So where to begin?

> Give thanks to Yahweh, call on His name;
> proclaim His deeds among the peoples.
> Sing to Him, sing praise to Him;
> tell about all His wonderful works!
> Psalm 105:1-2 (HCSB)

First of all, just do it. When there is an opportunity to sing for Jesus, sing with all your heart! There doesn't have to be a good band. It doesn't have be a style of music you enjoy. You don't have to be a good singer. Just give God the best of what you have, setting aside distractions and worry, and simply worshiping the God who promises to be present with us.

Second, worshiping with your words isn't only about singing. **Just like the altars of the Old Testament, our words are both a place of worship before God and a monument for others to witness.** The words you speak, all of your conversations, carry the power to awaken hearts and point people to Jesus.

You may have heard it said, "Preach the Gospel wherever you go, and if necessary, use words." That's a fine enough sentiment for encouraging people to live out their faith in their actions and not only their words, but it's certainly not a quote from the Bible. The Bible is clear in the many commands and commissions throughout the Old and New Testaments: we *must* use our words. We must "proclaim His deeds" and "tell about all His wonderful works." This includes both telling the story of Jesus and telling your own story of how He has changed your life.

Sharing your testimony is an act of worship, and God is glorified every time you do it. You might be thinking, "Well, I don't have much of a testimony to share." You may be like me, having grown up in a Christian home, come to faith at an age so early you barely remember, and lived a relatively uneventful life. That's okay. You still have things to be thankful for. You can still tell those around you about how God has provided for your finances. You can still share how He got you through a season of pain and loss. You can still share how reading a particular Bible passage encouraged you when you were down. You can still share the joy of feeling the Holy Spirit's presence when you worship. You can still share how God helped you make a tough decision. You can still share how God has forgiven you. **Every single blessing God has ever provided to you is an opportunity to testify of His goodness.**

I can promise you this: the more you tell your testimonies, the more testimonies you will have to share. The more you sing of God's goodness, the more of His goodness you will experience. The more you worship God with your words, the more words He will give you to pour out in worship. For we go from glory to glory (2 Corinthians 3:18).

God deserves your words. Ultimately, your words, like every other aspect of your life, give worship to something; and you have the choice: you can use them to worship Jesus or you can use them to worship something not nearly as worthy.

May we choose to worship Jesus with every utterance from our lips, for contained in our words is the power to bring both life and death (Proverbs 18:21). Choose life every day.

Think back to John the Baptist, who Jesus said was the greatest man ever born under the Old Covenant. Why did Jesus highlight John in such a dramatic way?

> So they asked him, "Why then do you baptize if you aren't the Messiah, or Elijah, or the Prophet?"
>
> "I baptize with water," John answered them. "Someone stands among you, but you don't know Him. He is the One coming after me, whose sandal strap I'm not worthy to untie."
>
> All this happened in Bethany across the Jordan, where John was baptizing.
>
> **The next day John saw Jesus coming toward him and said, "Here is the Lamb of God, who takes away the sin of the world!** This is the One I told you about: 'After me comes a man who has surpassed me, because He existed before me.' I didn't know Him, but I came baptizing with water so He might be revealed to Israel."
>
> And John testified, "I watched the Spirit descending from heaven like a dove, and He rested on Him. I didn't know Him, but He who sent me to baptize with water told me, 'The One you see the Spirit descending and resting on — He is the One who baptizes with the Holy Spirit.' **I have seen and testified that He is the Son of God!** "
>
> Again the next day, John was standing with two of his disciples. **When he saw Jesus passing by, he said, "Look! The Lamb of God!"**

John 1:25-35 (HCSB)

John was the first to begin preaching "the kingdom of Heaven has come near," which was the message that Jesus would give to His disciples. John did this because the Holy Spirit testified within him that he would see the Messiah. In the passage above, John has an experience that's actually similar to the men and women at the synagogue in Nazareth. He saw Jesus—he beheld Him. But unlike the mob that tried to throw Jesus off the cliff, John responded to the Holy Spirit by stepping out in faith and proclaiming the Truth with his words.

"Here is the Lamb of God, who takes away the sins of the world!" John saw Him. He proclaimed Him. He served Him. And he never stopped proclaiming. Even when John was in prison, awaiting his death, he did not allow his doubts to compromise his message (Matthew 11). Instead of abandoning his faith, John sent word through his disciples to Jesus to inquire. If you ever find yourself doubting the Gospel you were once certain was true, don't allow it to compromise your faith. Don't allow doubt to erode the story God has given you. Instead, follow John's example and send word to Jesus. Allow Jesus to change your perspective by pointing to the true evidence.

When Jesus said that the least of us in the kingdom would be greater than John, it didn't mean that our mission was any different than John's. It simply means that we now have the opportunity to live and tell the rest of the story, something John did not get to see before he was executed. We have the baptism of the Holy Spirit that John prophesied but did not live to experience. Our assignment, however, is the same: behold the Messiah, proclaim Him, serve Him. And, like John, we must never change the subject until we die.

10 IN DEED

I have this burning desire deep within me to see and experience revival. I'm not just talking about a long weekend of church services (although, I do love being a part of those). I'm talking about a true movement of the Holy Spirit in which millions upon millions of lives are radically saved by Jesus Christ and adopted into the Family of God. It's what I pray for constantly. It's what I live for.

One day, not that long ago, I was walking my dog around our neighborhood in Nashville, Tennessee, praying for revival to come again to the United States. As I thought about the political climate in our country and the moral collapse happening in my own generation, I turned my heart to God, recognizing that without His grace and power, we're hopeless to escape the pit we've dug for ourselves.

"God, we need you so desperately," I prayed. "Please pour out your Spirit on America. We need another Great Awakening!"

Suddenly, I heard God speak to my heart in clear, unambiguous words, "Revival in your country starts with revival in your city." I got excited!

"Yes, God! Bring revival here to Nashville! Let the Gospel

be manifest so powerfully in my city that it ripples outward to the rest of the country."

God spoke again, "Revival in your city starts with revival in your neighborhood." This time, I knew that God wasn't just asking me to pray a generic prayer for Him to do something. It was an invitation for me to join Him in what I was praying for, but I didn't have a clue where to begin.

"How, Lord?" I asked. "How do I reach my neighborhood with the Gospel? Where should I begin?"

As I walked back toward my house, a stillness came over me. There were no more specific words from God, but an idea began to form in my head. I imagined my wife Hannah and I bringing baked goods to our neighbors and telling them that we were praying for them. I also felt like we should bring our baked gifts on real plates, so that when they finished eating, they would return the plates to us, and we might have another opportunity to share the love of Jesus with them. It was just a simple idea, but I was extraordinarily excited about it because it came attached to the hope of revival.

I couldn't wait to share with Hannah what God had told me, but when I told her the whole story, she was far less enthusiastic than I was. Hannah is, by nature, a quiet person who keeps to herself and doesn't usually go our of her way to talk to strangers. I knew that the prospect of knocking on strangers' doors and striking up a conversation was not something she would be particularly jazzed about.

She told me with a frown, "That's all fine, but I think it's kind of annoying that you've got this plan you think is from God that involves me baking." I was undeterred, the bright hope of reaching our neighborhood with Jesus' love had already taken root in my heart.

"I understand, but don't worry about that," I replied as gently as I knew how. "Just pray about it. If you don't feel like this is something God is also asking you to do, then I'll learn to bake and do it by myself. But please, just ask God to tell you if this is something you should participate in."

Hannah agreed to pray about it, and a few days later she came back to me and said, "I've been asking God about your idea, and I think we should do it." I was energized and replied with a high five!

We began to discuss whom we should visit first. Hannah suggested a couple right around the corner from us, saying that those were the first people her heart was drawn toward. We didn't know their names and had only said "hello" a few times in passing. From a bumper sticker and a t-shirt one of them wore once, we had the vague notion that they might already be Christians, but perhaps that was a good place to begin. I thought this would be a safe, low-risk test run. If they already know Jesus, we'll just encourage them, and at the same time, it will build up our confidence in the whole process.

That week, we began praying for those neighbors, and after several days of prayer, Hannah woke up early one morning and made banana bread. We sat in our living room together and gave thanks for them, praying that God would be with us as we visited and shared the simple gift of baked goods.

"God, show us Your heart for them," we prayed. "Teach us to love them the way You love them. Help us to be good stewards of the opportunities you've given us in this neighborhood so that we might see your kingdom come here in our city."

After we finished praying together, I went to my office and continued to pray for them during my quiet time with God. I asked the Lord, "Father, if there's something we're supposed to do or say when we're there, would you just speak to my heart?"

God's answer came in a single word, like a thought in my mind, but I knew it wasn't my own thought. I heard Him say the word "greater." I snapped to attention and physically leaned in, trying to listen to what the Holy Spirit was saying.

Then, I heard the word, "Charlotte."

Confused, I literally asked aloud, "Lord, could you elaborate?"

God whispered clearly, "They've seen me do good things in the past, but I'm getting ready to do something greater." Excitement rushed into my heart like a flood of sunlight! I suddenly knew that God had a specific purpose for us visiting these particular neighbors.

But then, I paused. "What about 'Charlotte'? I don't know what that means…"

I waited for an answer, but God said nothing. Total silence. I was bewildered. It seemed so clear when He said it. Like a song that gets stuck in your head, I couldn't shake the word from my mind. Charlotte. What in the world did it mean?

I went to Hannah and asked, "Did God tell you anything about our neighbors?" I was hoping that perhaps God had spoken the same words to her. That would have made me feel much better about the whole situation.

"Nope," was her simple reply. Perplexed, I pondered it all day long. I knew that God said something great was on the way for this family, and it had something to do with Charlotte. Not wanting to be talked out of how sure I was that I had heard God speak, I didn't even tell Hannah about it. I was afraid she wouldn't understand or just think I was going nuts! But then again, I felt like maybe I was going nuts.

My mind grasped for possible meanings. *Maybe they went to Charlotte, North Carolina, and God did something good there, and what He's getting ready to do is even greater.* That sounded reasonable…

"Am I supposed to say this out loud to them? I don't even know how to bring it up!" I told God. God remained silent, and I grew anxious. I wanted to go ahead and get the whole thing over with, but Hannah said we should wait until the evening before bringing the banana bread over. So, I paced around the house all day, unable to escape the words "greater" and "Charlotte" that played over and over again in my mind.

Finally, it was time to head down the street and around the corner to see our neighbors. I knew that God was with us, but my heart pounded in my chest. We arrived and knocked on the front door, banana bread in hand. When the woman opened the door, we could see the furniture in their living room was haphazardly piled in the middle of the room.

"I'm so sorry!" our neighbor told us. "My husband and I are rearranging everything. We're trying to make more space in here. You caught us at a bad time!"

"That's okay," Hannah and I said. "We just came to bring you some bread and tell you that we're so thankful to have you as our neighbors. We've been praying for you."

The lady and her husband were visibly moved by our gesture of kindness. "Thank you so much! That's really amazing. How nice of you two!"

"Is there anything in particular that we can be in prayer about for you?" I asked.

"Actually, yes there is," she said. "Our niece, who just turned 18 and is pregnant, is about to move in with us. That's why we've got all the furniture moved around."

Without even thinking, before I could stop myself, I blurted out, "Is her name Charlotte?" There it went! No turning back now!

"Yeah, it is!" She was puzzled. "How did you know that?"

My eyes grew wide with amazement at God's incredible power, and I could barely contain my excitement! "I was praying for you this morning, and I heard God say the name 'Charlotte,' but I didn't know what it meant! I've been walking around all day confused about it!"

They both gasped at what they were hearing. "I just got chills all over!" said the woman!

"Oh, here's the good part..." I said. "God also said that you guys have experienced good things in the past, but what He's getting ready to do is even greater. Wow! He loves you so much! I know God is *all about* what you are doing right now, and He loves Charlotte so much that He told me her name before I even knew who she was."

We all paused and stood there in silence. It was a holy moment. Then we joined hands together and prayed for them as they prepared to welcome Charlotte and her new baby into their home. Hannah and I went home rejoicing in what God had just done!

We sat across the kitchen table from each other processing the sequence of events. If God hadn't given me the idea on my walk... If Hannah hadn't said "yes" to God... If she hadn't been drawn to that particular couple... If I hadn't asked God to speak to me... If I hadn't listened... Clearly, God had set us up for success! Without God, there was no possible explanation for what had just transpired.

"You know, I have not been asking God to prove Himself to me. I really haven't," I told Hannah. "I already believed in Him with my whole heart. But after that...I am *all in!* There's no way we could ever turn back!"

Since that day, Hannah and I have continued to bring baked goods to people in our neighborhood. God has led us into opportunity after opportunity to show His love. We have prayed for the sick. We have encouraged with our words and with sweet treats. We have shared the Gospel with neighbors who sat desperate and lonely in their living rooms. We have experienced the wonderful kindness of strangers and the immeasurable goodness of God...all through the simple act of giving food.

We can worship God with all our words and all our mind,

but at the end of the day, without putting those things into action, we come up far short of God's design for our lives. Worshiping the Lord with our deeds is where the rubber meets the road. It's where the invisible (your character, your integrity, the life you cultivate in the secret place) meets the visible (your gifts, ability, and talents).

Even in the Old Testament, God made it clear that obedience to His commands are far sweeter worship than any sacrifice (1 Samuel 15:22). We can go to church and sing passionately with hearts full of faith, but without action behind our words, we're merely paying lip service to God. What God desires is a life laid down in surrender, nothing held back from His purposes. We can sing "I surrender all" a million times, but unless we walk out the door and actually give Jesus our every action, we're just singing empty words. God has a plan for our lives that's so much bigger than singing songs, much bigger than a good philosophy, much better than a nice moral code.

Have you ever wondered about your life's purpose here on this earth? Why are you here? It's a good question to ask. A lot of people spend years and years of their life wandering about aimlessly trying to answer that question. As disciples of Jesus, however, we already have an answer.

> You are the salt of the earth. But if the salt should lose its taste, how can it be made salty? It's no longer good for anything but to be thrown out and trampled on by men.

> You are the light of the world. A city situated on a hill cannot be hidden. No one lights a lamp and puts it under a basket, but rather on a lampstand, and it gives light for all who are in the house. In the same way, let your light shine before men, so that they may see your good works and give glory to your Father in heaven.
> Matthew 5:13-16 (HCSB)

I rather like how Eugene Peterson paraphrased verse 13 in *The Message* Bible:

> Let me tell you why you are here. You're here to be salt-seasoning that brings out the God-flavors of this earth. If you lose your saltiness, how will people taste godliness? You've lost your usefulness and will end up in the garbage.
> Matthew 5:13 (The Message)

Salt and light. That's why you're here, to be for the world what they could never possibly experience without Jesus Christ. You carry the Holy Spirit inside of you everywhere you go, and are commissioned to co-labor with Christ in His ministry to draw others to Himself, giving them the opportunity to both "taste and see" that He is deeply, perfectly good. We'll talk about being light in chapter 12; but for now, let's focus on what it means to be salt.

Cooking is pastime both my wife and I enjoy very much. Something every cook learns early on is that salt is a "flavor enhancer." A little bit of salt added to bland food can suddenly cause the entire dish to come alive. It helps separate flavors and make them distinct and vibrant. A dish full of spices but no salt tastes muddled and uninviting, but salt enhances the flavor of each ingredient, bringing so much subtlety and nuance that often fewer ingredients are needed to make a dish explode with flavor.

As Christians, we are called to live in a way that brings vibrancy and flavor everywhere we go. Like Joseph in Pharaoh's palace, we're called to bring the flavor of Heaven to a world in famine. Like Daniel serving in Nebuchadnezzar's court, we're called to bring definition and meaning to things that no one outside of Christ can understand. We are to recognize that God created each and every person with a unique fingerprint, a unique reflection of His image (whether they know Him or not), and season them with the Holy Spirit who lives within us. We are tasked with calling people into their destiny as God's creation, drawing them in to be the children they were designed to be.

The metaphor of salt goes even deeper. In addition to bringing flavor, salt is also a picture of God's kingdom advancing to destroy the works of Satan. In ancient times, when an enemy city was to be completely destroyed, often the conquering army would scorch the ground and pour salt over it so that nothing would ever grow there again (Judges 9:45). As we worship Jesus with our actions, we advance against the darkness, tearing down the strongholds of the enemy.

The Apostle Paul teaches us to daily clothe ourselves for battle, not against other people but against the armies of darkness that battle against them (Ephesians 6:11-12). You might be thinking to yourself that spiritual warfare is something that pastors or missionaries do, but notice what Paul describes as the armor of God. It's made of up things that every Christian is called to, not just those in vocational ministry:

> Stand, therefore,
> with truth like a belt around your waist,
> righteousness like armor on your chest,
> and your feet sandaled with readiness
> for the gospel of peace.
> In every situation take the shield of faith,
> and with it you will be able to extinguish
> all the flaming arrows of the evil one.
> Take the helmet of salvation,
> and the sword of the Spirit,
> which is God's word.
>
> Pray at all times in the Spirit with every prayer
> and request, and stay alert in this with all
> perseverance and intercession for all the saints.
> Ephesians 6:14-18 (HCSB)

To be the salt of the earth is to clothe yourself with truth, righteousness, peace, faith, salvation, and the Word. To be salt is to intercede in prayer for your fellow brothers and sisters in Christ. The context of this passage in Ephesians 6 is fascinating because it doesn't come out of deep, heady philosophy but the most practical instructions to the Church. Children, obey your parents. Fathers, train your children in the ways of God. Servants, work for your masters as if you were working for God Himself. Masters, treat your servants with the same kind of favor and generosity as God gives us. The battleground isn't just the four walls of the Church or a foreign mission field but the everyday life that each of us lives.

What would it look like if you went to your job every day, and, instead of simply fulfilling the requirements in order to get your paycheck, you poured your full energy into every task as if you were serving Jesus Himself? What would it look like if you went to battle against apathy, mediocrity, and selfish ambition in your work? Do you think your employer or clients would take notice? I have many friends whose biggest opportunities to share the Gospel with others came because they worked harder and with more integrity at their jobs than any of their co-workers.

As Christians, we no longer work secular, meaningless jobs but take every opportunity to worship the Lord in our actions. Whatever you are doing, do it with all of your might as an act of holy worship before God. Even if your employer doesn't notice or reward you for your efforts, know that God receives your actions as a fragrant act of worship and will reward you with the the riches of Heaven (Colossians 3:23).

In the Bible, salt is also a picture of healing and restoration. We see this depicted in a story from the prophet Elisha's life:

> Then the men of the city said to Elisha, "Even though our lord can see that the city's location is good, the water is bad and the land unfruitful."
>
> He replied, "Bring me a new bowl and put salt in it."
>
> After they had brought him one, Elisha went out to the spring of water, threw salt in it, and said, "This is what the Lord says: 'I have healed this water. No

longer will death or unfruitfulness result from it.' "
2 Kings 2:19-20 (HCSB)

Elisha was among the Nazirites who lived a consecrated life, set apart from the ordinary before God in constant prayer and fasting. Just like he brought restoration to the spring by pouring salt in it, we are called to bring restoration and life to places poisoned and stagnate. We are new creations, filled with the Holy Spirit, like the new bowl of salt Elisha requested to pour into the poisoned spring. Because the same Holy Spirit that raised Jesus from the dead lives inside us, we have the same commission as Jesus to go and bring life where there is death.

The book of Isaiah puts it this way:

> Isn't the fast I choose:
> To break the chains of wickedness,
> to untie the ropes of the yoke,
> to set the oppressed free,
> and to tear off every yoke?
> Is it not to share your bread with the hungry,
> to bring the poor and homeless into your house,
> to clothe the naked when you see him,
> and not to ignore your own flesh and blood?
> Then your light will appear like the dawn,
> and your recovery will come quickly.
> Your righteousness will go before you,
> and the Lord's glory will be your rear guard.
> Isaiah 58:6-8 (HCSB)

Rather than mere symbolic acts of devotion (like fasting from food), the worship that God desires is for us to bring redemption to broken people. If we sing great songs of praise to God but don't also share what we have with the poor, our words are empty. If we fast from food or drink but don't also work to bring about heavenly justice in the world, our actions are meaningless. Earlier in Isaiah's prophecy, God scolded the Israelites saying that they worship only with their lips, but their hearts were far away (Isaiah 29:13). In the New

Testament, the Apostle Paul writes that even the most angelic singing we can muster without the love of Christ in action rings harsh in God's ears like a clanging cymbal (1 Corinthians 13:1).

Every Christian is called to bring healing and hope to the world. If you love Jesus and have committed your life to following Him, you have already been qualified to carry out God's commission to preach the Gospel, heal the sick, and bring freedom to the oppressed. Now, we must steward those things carefully through diligent practice and faithful obedience.

> What good is it, my brothers, if someone says he has faith but does not have works? Can his faith save him?
>
> If a brother or sister is without clothes and lacks daily food and one of you says to them, "Go in peace, keep warm, and eat well," but you don't give them what the body needs, what good is it? In the same way faith, if it doesn't have works, is dead by itself.
> James 2:14-15 (HCSB)

Think back to the story I told about myself in chapter 2, the one where I disobeyed God and didn't pray with the woman with carpal tunnel syndrome. At the time, my faith in God and His plan for my life was so small that I looked for excuses to get out of what He was telling me to do. Being a worship leader was all well and good, but without the action to reach outside my comfort zone, my faith was crippled. Thanks to God's amazing grace, I have learned to marry the faith I proclaim with my mouth to the actions I take every day.

I have found that the single biggest factor in building faith is simply obedience to God. Whatever God is asking of me, the quicker I obey, the less likely I am to falter and doubt. The quicker I say "yes" to God and put my faith into action, the less likely I am to disobey. There comes frequently the moment where we must take a leap of faith—risking embarrassment, failure, security, or vulnerability—but God's goodness on the other side of the leap is always worth it!

Even if we come up short of a perfect outcome (and that *certainly* will happen), the knowledge that we obeyed and that God is pleased with our obedience, is far better than having remained in our comfort zone or disobeyed. Remember Joseph in the Bible, who honored God by not sleeping with Potiphar's wife, found himself in prison for being faithful to God's righteousness. He must have felt like a total failure, but in reality, God was setting him up for even greater success! God was honored by Joseph's obedience and was unhindered by the circumstances it led to.

Whether you carry out obedience in something that seems important like doing missions work or something that seems ordinary like babysitting someone's kids, God is honored by the heart that goes behind it. Don't forget the parable of the talents that Jesus told in Matthew 25: to each servant the master gave a different amount to steward while he was away. The two servants who received more multiplied what the master had given them, but the one who received little buried his in the ground because he was afraid to take a risk. The master honored the servants who used what was given to them but sharply reprimanded the lazy servant who did not use his talent. Be faithful with where God has placed you right now; and in time, He will trust you with even greater responsibility.

Be quick to obey when you feel God stirring your heart to action. I have found that the more time I spend questioning the command God has given, the more likely I am to disobey. The more time I spend wondering if I heard the voice of the Holy Spirit accurately, the more likely I am to miss out on being a part of His amazing plan.

If you're not sure if what you're feeling led to do is from the Lord, remember this: **we all have different spiritual gifts to put into action, but the fruit by which we measure them is the same.** Something my wife and I frequently do to help us discern if a call to action is from God is run it through the Fruit of the Spirit like a check-list:

- Is what I'm feeling led to do loving?
- Can I do this joyfully and with a good attitude?
- Will what I'm feeling led to do bring peace to others? (Remember, the peace we're talking about here is more than just emotion or lack of nervousness. Real peace is the presence of Jesus, the Peacemaker.)
- Is what I'm feeling led to do patient, or am I simply trying to speed up something I'm tired of waiting on?
- Is what I'm feeling led to do kind?
- Is what I'm feeling led to do self-seeking? Would I be doing this to get noticed, or would it be okay if nobody knew it was me who did it?
- Is what I'm feeling led to do good? Does it line up with God's Word?
- Does what I'm feeling led to do take faith in Someone bigger than myself? Am I being faithful to what is written in God's Word? Will it build up faith in others?
- Is what I'm feeling led to do gentle? Can I do it in a way that lifts someone up instead of tearing them down?
- Is what I'm feeling led to do self-controlled? Is this really about feeding my own desires and wants?

If you can get through the whole list, and everything checks out, go for it! Take a risk and see what God does with your faith in action. These are truly the "God flavors" that we're called to bring to the world! Paul says "against such things there is no law" (Galatians 5:23).

If you find yourself stuck or unable to discern if what you're hearing is from the Lord, take it to Him in prayer. If you're still confused or unsure, bring what's on your heart to your Pastor or church elders. Ask them to help you pray and discern if what you're feeling led to do is from God.

My wife Hannah weighed all those kinds of things in her heart as she prayed about bringing baked goods to our neighbors; and in the end, even though she felt anxious about talking to strangers, she decided to step out in faith and trust that God was in the plan.

Here's an example from my own life: I was at a Christian concert last year, and there was a man next to me whom I had never met. As we sang worship songs together, I felt like the Lord was leading me to pray for the man and that he was wrestling with anxiety. I asked God if I was supposed to simply pray for the man silently or if I should speak to him about it. In my heart, I felt like the Holy Spirit was asking me to talk to him, but when I ran it through the Fruit of the Spirit checklist, I got stuck on "gentleness."

I thought that it might be really harsh if I just turned to someone I had never met and asked, "Excuse me. Are you struggling with anxiety?" Doing so seemed like it might actually make his problem worse rather than better. So, I prayed to God and asked Him to show me how I might share a message of peace to this man in a gentle way. As soon as I prayed about it, the Lord brought a specific Bible verse to mind:

> "Don't worry about anything, but in everything, through prayer and petition with thanksgiving, let your requests be made known to God."
> Philippians 4:6 (HCSB)

Immediately, I knew that I could share this verse with him in a gentle way, without being harsh or accusatory. As a matter of fact, many years earlier, a stranger had written this very verse on a note card and given it to me, and that person could not have possibly had better timing! At that time in my life, I was worried about all sorts of things, and Philippians 4:6 was what my soul desperately needed to hear. I remembered the relief it gave me and the confidence that God was with me, and this filled my heart with faith that sharing this Scripture was the right thing to do.

As soon as the concert was over, I went to the man and told him, "This might be a little strange, but as we were worshiping, I felt like God gave me a Bible verse for you. Is it okay if I share it with you?"

"Really?" he asked, surprised but not put off. "That'd be

great. Tell me."

I read him the verse and said, "I don't know if you've been struggling with anxiety, but I know that God cares about all the details. You can bring everything to him in prayer, and know that He's got your back."

I asked if any of that made any sense to him, and he replied, "Wow! More than you could possibly know! Thank you!"

Actions like that are so simple, and any follower of Jesus can do them. Our time in the secret place prepares us for service, and seeing God use our service gives us fuel to worship Jesus all over again! The small things prepare our hearts for bigger callings and greater acts of service, and when we are faithful in them, we find that obedience in the big things isn't nearly as intimidating because we've already built up our courage.

Worshiping God with your actions doesn't require any special directive from Heaven. I've used a few stories from my life as examples, but not every calling starts with a specific prompting of the Holy Spirit. Perhaps you're ready to serve God, but you're unsure where to start. The answer is simple: start with what God has placed in front of you.

There are certain places where we can be confident that we will always find the Lord. For example, God has called every Christian to serve the poor. The command is all throughout the Bible, and Jesus said we will find the kingdom of God with the poor (Luke 6:20). Every Christian is called to serve widows and orphans. Serving them is pure and undefiled worship before God (James 1:27). Every Christian is called to care for the sick. Jesus says that as we do these things for others, it is the same as serving Himself:

> For I was hungry
> and you gave Me something to eat;
> I was thirsty
> and you gave Me something to drink;

> I was a stranger and you took Me in;
> I was naked and you clothed Me;
> I was sick and you took care of Me;
> I was in prison and you visited Me.'
>
> Then the righteous will answer Him, 'Lord, when did we see You hungry and feed You, or thirsty and give You something to drink? When did we see You a stranger and take You in, or without clothes and clothe You? When did we see You sick, or in prison, and visit You?'
>
> And the King will answer them, 'I assure you: Whatever you did for one of the least of these brothers of Mine, you did for Me.'
> Matthew 25:35-40 (HCSB)

Last year, Hannah and I served with a group at a day care facility for teenagers and adults with intellectual disabilities. Before going in the facility to meet our new friends, the director met with us outside and read that passage from Matthew 25. She told us that serving and being the hands and feet of Jesus was an honorable thing, but as we served, make sure to recognize that Jesus was already with the people there. That simple statement changed our perspectives forever.

Throughout the day, as we helped our friends eat, exercise, play, and make crafts, we were full of awareness that we were serving Jesus. As I helped a young woman cut salt-dough with a cookie cutter, steadying her hands for her because she lacked muscle control, I felt the wonder and awe of knowing that I was steadying Jesus' hands. As we danced with our friends during recreation and exercise time, we were filled with immeasurable joy from the knowledge that we were dancing with Jesus. Instead of leaving depleted from working hard (and we did work hard!), we left full, knowing that we had just spent time with Jesus.

I have met Jesus on construction sites while hanging drywall. I have met Him cleaning houses after a flood. I have met Him on airplanes and in waiting rooms. I have met Jesus in prison cell blocks. I have met Him in churches and soup kitchens. I have met Him at universities and vacation Bible schools. I have met Him in living rooms and back yards. I have met Him in restaurants and grocery stores. If we seek Him, we will find Him.

It is not difficult to find opportunities to serve. Serve in your local church, at a homeless shelter, a missions trip, or simply find a neighbor in need. It's not nearly as important *where* you start as much as that you start *somewhere*. However, keep in mind that this isn't just a box to check off but a lifestyle we are called to live until we go home to be with Jesus for eternity in Heaven. Until that day, we live to be His kingdom here on earth.

There is no gift that you can give God that is too extravagant. No outpouring of worship you could bring could possibly outmeasure what He deserves. Jesus is worth it all and then some.

Not everyone will appreciate an extravagant act of worship. King David's wife Michal was appalled at how undignified he appeared dancing before the Ark of the Covenant as it made its way into Jerusalem:

> When David returned home to bless his household, Saul's daughter Michal came out to meet him. "How the king of Israel honored himself today! " she said. "He exposed himself today in the sight of the slave girls of his subjects like a vulgar person would expose himself."
>
> David replied to Michal, "I was dancing before the Lord who chose me over your father and his whole family to appoint me ruler over the Lord's people Israel. I will celebrate before the Lord, and I will humble myself even more and humiliate myself."
> 2 Samuel 6:20-22 (HCSB)

Sometimes we even find Michal's attitude toward worship in the church. People who worship with great abandon are often dismissed as irreverent or disorderly. But if we look at David's example, we see that shedding dignity and worshiping with great passion was actually the *most reverent* posture to take before the presence of the Lord.

Christians are often mocked, ridiculed, and persecuted for living a life of devotion to Christ, but we can be confident that God never abandons us when we face opposition. As a matter of fact, the Bible promises that God's glory will rest upon you any time you are ridiculed for the sake of Christ (1 Peter 4:12-14). This doesn't mean that we walk around with a chip on our shoulder, looking for opposition. The Apostle Paul wrote unequivocally that we should "bless those who persecute" us (Romans 12:14). Not only do we have the promise that God will be with us, but we also have the hope that God might use our blessing to melt the heart of our persecutors and draw them to Himself. Even the Roman soldiers who presided over Jesus' crucifixion ended up recognizing that He was the Son of God (Matthew 27:54).

The Devil hates passionate acts of worship, but he is powerless to stop it if we refuse to allow him to intimidate us. It was actually a radical and extravagant act of worship that served as the final straw before Judas betrayed Jesus into the hands of the Pharisees.

> While Jesus was in Bethany at the house of Simon, a man who had a serious skin disease, a woman approached Him with an alabaster jar of very expensive fragrant oil. She poured it on His head as He was reclining at the table. When the disciples saw it, they were indignant. "Why this waste?" they asked. "This might have been sold for a great deal and given to the poor."
>
> But Jesus, aware of this, said to them, "Why are you bothering this woman? She has done a noble

> thing for Me. You always have the poor with you, but you do not always have Me. By pouring this fragrant oil on My body, she has prepared Me for burial. **I assure you: Wherever this gospel is proclaimed in the whole world, what this woman has done will also be told in memory of her."**
>
> Then one of the Twelve — the man called Judas Iscariot — went to the chief priests and said, "What are you willing to give me if I hand Him over to you?" So they weighed out 30 pieces of silver for him. And from that time he started looking for a good opportunity to betray Him.
> Matthew 26:6-16 (HCSB)

We can choose to be timid. We can choose to hold onto dignity and pride. We can choose to stay in our comfort zones. Or we can make it our regular practice to pour everything in our lives out as a fragrant offering onto Jesus. Oh, to give Him the kind of worship that glorifies Him for generations to come!

Worship without deeds of service is always incomplete, just as under the Old Testament law, no burnt offering was to be given without salt:

> You are to season each of your grain offerings with salt; you must not omit from your grain offering the salt of the covenant with your God. You are to present salt with each of your offerings.
> Leviticus 2:13 (HCSB)

Let your every action be the salt that seasons your life of worship before God, in view of the world around you. Unify your heart of worship as one holy and pleasing sacrifice before the Lord. Worship Him in thought, word, and deed. Do it passionately, extravagantly, no matter what the cost. The reward is Jesus Himself, and there can be nothing greater!

11 THE WILDERNESS

Moses had some of the most profound experiences with God of any person in human history. He was a man who the Bible says spoke with God "face to face, just as a man speaks to his friend" (Exodus 33:11). He once spent two 40-day periods, back to back, with no food or water, but his bodily health was sustained because of the presence of God. As a matter of fact, at the end of his life, we are told that Moses was still strong and his eyes were as sharp as ever (Deuteronomy 34:7), as if the time he spent face to face with God had such a profound effect on his body that he no longer aged! This was the man to whom God granted the request that he might see His glory, a glory so profound and powerful that Moses could not stare at it directly but had to be covered by the hand of God until He had finished passing in front of him (Exodus 33:17-23).

Keeping all this in mind about Moses, how is it that he wavered so disastrously in his faith that he was not allowed to enter the Promised Land? For the third time since the Israelites entered the wilderness (the first was in Exodus 15, the second in Exodus 17), Moses found himself leading thirsty people with no sign of water anywhere in sight. The people complained against Moses and disregarded all that God had already done for them, including miraculously provide them with water twice before. The Israelites described the wilderness they were in as an "evil place," even though it was the Lord who had led them there (Numbers 20:1-5). Faced again with insurrection, Moses and Aaron went to seek a solution from the Lord.

> Then Moses and Aaron went from the presence of the assembly to the doorway of the tent of meeting. They fell down with their faces to the ground, and the glory of the Lord appeared to them. The Lord spoke to Moses, "Take the staff and assemble the community. **You and your brother Aaron are to speak to the rock while they watch, and it will yield its water.** You will bring out water for them from the rock and provide drink for the community and their livestock."
>
> So Moses took the staff from the Lord's presence just as He had commanded him. Moses and Aaron summoned the assembly in front of the rock, and Moses said to them, "Listen, you rebels! Must we bring water out of this rock for you? " **Then Moses raised his hand and struck the rock twice with his staff, so that a great amount of water gushed out, and the community and their livestock drank**.
>
> But the Lord said to Moses and Aaron, "Because you did not trust Me to show My holiness in the sight of the Israelites, you will not bring this assembly into the land I have given them." These are the waters of Meribah, where the Israelites quarreled with the Lord, and He showed His holiness to them.
> Numbers 20:2-13 (HCSB)

Because of his disobedience, Moses didn't get to enter the Promised Land and only saw it from a distance before Joshua led the Israelites in. So what happened? How did Moses go from the mountain top before the glory of God to being overwhelmed in the depths of doubt?

We see similar examples of failure quite often don't we? Celebrities and politicians who are on top of the world have public meltdowns and scandals. Church leaders who once seemed to have everything going for them suddenly collapse into disobedience and sin. Mentors and heroes we trusted and admired disappoint us by violating every principle they taught us. In our own lives, sin and doubt have a way of creeping up on us, even after we've celebrated a milestone in our life with Jesus.

If you've been around the Church for any length of time, you may have had a "mountain top" experience yourself, a time when God seemed closer than your very skin, when nothing was more exciting or fulfilling than worshiping or reading the Word. Sometimes we experience a significant breakthrough in our faith, an answered prayer, or a special time of fellowship with God that leaves us *sure* that He is near. Churches may experience a move of the Spirit that brings revival, and for a season, there seem to be no boundaries on faith and expectation. Young people frequently experience these spiritual highs at church summer camps or retreats.

But then, inevitably, we come down off the mountain top and life seems…ordinary. The traditional liturgical church calendar that many churches around the world follow actually has a season between Epiphany and Lent called "Ordinary Time." Throughout life, there seems to be quite a lot of ordinary time, doesn't there?

Worse yet, sometimes we find ourselves somewhere below ordinary in unfamiliar, barren territory, where faith feels like a grinding struggle, and the promises of God suddenly seem out of our grasp. This is the wilderness. But are we really supposed leave the glory we experienced on the mountain top behind? Are movements of the Spirit, both personal and church revivals, intended to be temporary and only for short seasons? I don't believe so.

If you search through the Bible, you will find a repeating pattern in virtually every major character's life. Somewhere between God's promise and the fulfillment of it is a season spent in the wilderness. In many stories, we read about a *literal* wilderness; but always, there comes a time when faith is put to the test before the men and women of God step into their destiny.

Abraham waited 25 years between God's promise that he would father a great nation and when his son Isaac was born. Joseph had dreams of greatness from God but spent years in slavery before becoming Pharaoh's second in command over Egypt. After the Prophet Samuel anointed him as the next king of Israel, David went back to the sheep fields and then spent years in the wilderness running from King Saul before the prophecy came to fulfillment. Elijah was reduced from conquering the false prophets of Baal on the mountain top to wasting away in the wilderness with only God's miraculous provision of food from ravens sustaining him. John the Baptist actually spent most of his life in the wilderness, with the promise that he would see the Messiah, before finally baptizing Jesus in the Jordan River. After his encounter with Jesus on the road to Damascus, Paul spent three years in the wilderness before his ministry as an apostle started.

There is much we can learn from each of these great stories, but let's focus on the two wilderness stories at the heart of the Biblical narrative: the nation of Israel's 40 years of wandering after deliverance from Egypt and Jesus' 40 days of fasting and prayer in the wilderness after His baptism.

In many respects, the account of the Israelites in Exodus, Leviticus, Numbers, and Deuteronomy is as heartbreaking as it is awe-inspiring. After 400 years of slavery in Egypt, Moses led God's chosen people to liberty through some of the most dramatic expressions of God's power ever recorded. Yet virtually every step of the journey, the Israelites seemed to forget how far God had already brought them and were paralyzed by fear, doubt, and disobedience.

One of the most baffling figures in the narrative is Moses'

older brother Aaron, who stood by his side as the lead communicator during all of the 10 plagues in Egypt. Each step of the way, Aaron was more than just a first-hand witness of God's power but an active participant in the story. Still, as Moses met with God for 40 days on Mount Sinai, even as the entire mountain burned with the fire of God's radiant presence, Aaron was somehow persuaded to cast an idol for the Israelites to worship. How is it possible that standing in front of a flaming mountain, hearing the thunderous voice of God and feeling the ground shake beneath their feet, Aaron and the Israelites turned aside and created a golden calf to bow down to?

The sequence of events between Exodus 19 and Exodus 34 gives us clues as to where it all went wrong. When the Israelites had reached Mt. Sinai, God called Moses up the mountain to meet with Him, saying to the congregation, "Now if you will listen to Me and carefully keep My covenant, you will be My own possession" (Exodus 19:5). The people affirm that they will do all the Lord instructed, and God begins to give Moses instructions to prepare the people to hear His voice.

> The Lord said to Moses, "I am going to come to you in a dense cloud, so that the people will hear when I speak with you and will always believe you." Then Moses reported the people's words to the Lord.
> Exodus 19:9 (HCSB)

After three days of consecration, God appeared on the mountain, consuming it entirely in thick smoke and flames, shaking the ground with a violent earthquake. God spoke to Moses with a voice like thunder! The Lord called both Moses and Aaron to come up the mountain:

> And the Lord replied to him, "Go down and come back with Aaron. But the priests and the people must not break through to come up to the Lord, or He will break out in anger against them." So

> Moses went down to the people and told them.
> Exodus 19:24 (HCSB)

Then, God spoke the 10 Commandments (including "don't make idols for yourself"). What happens next is key:

> All the people witnessed the thunder and lightning, the sound of the trumpet, and the mountain surrounded by smoke. When the people saw it they trembled and stood at a distance. **"You speak to us, and we will listen," they said to Moses, "but don't let God speak to us, or we will die."**
>
> Moses responded to the people, "Don't be afraid, for God has come to test you, so that you will fear Him and will not sin." And the people remained standing at a distance as Moses approached the thick darkness where God was.
> Exodus 20:18-21 (HCSB)

I sincerely believe that this moment is where it all begins to unravel for Aaron and the Israelites. God gave the invitation for the entire congregation to hear His voice and issued instructions for how they were to prepare themselves. **But, when the time came to listen, the Israelites rejected the opportunity to hear directly from God.**

I have often puzzled over why the Israelites were so crippled by fear that they would pass on such a momentous invitation, even after God had delivered them from slavery in such miraculous fashion. At the heart of the matter is a fundamental misunderstanding (and therefore a distrust) of God's loving and merciful nature. This is affirmed several times throughout the Psalms, as we will see. Perhaps their distrust stemmed from the fact that the only experiences they had ever had with anyone claiming to be a "god" were the tyrannical pharaohs who brutally enslaved them. Or perhaps the sight of God's power highlighted the root of sin within their hearts, and they could not fathom why God might be merciful to them. Regardless, instead of taking God up on His offer to speak to them directly, they remained distant. In the wake of that decision to reject God's voice, God began to deliver the Levitical law.

However, it's not as though God only gave Aaron and the congregation only one opportunity. We see in Exodus 24, God calls Moses, Aaron, and scores of Israel's elders up the mountain to dine with Him! Again, they all affirmed their commitment to obey all God's instructions.

> Then Moses went up with Aaron, Nadab, and Abihu, and 70 of Israel's elders, and they saw the God of Israel. Beneath His feet was something like a pavement made of sapphire stone, as clear as the sky itself. **God did not harm the Israelite nobles; they saw Him, and they ate and drank.**
> Exodus 24:9-11 (HCSB)

What a meal that must have been! One more time, we catch a glimpse of God's true nature: "God did not harm the Israelite nobles" but instead invited them to dine with Him.

As the story continues, God keeps calling Moses higher up the mountain, deeper into his glorious presence, but none of the elders accompany him. Only one young man, Joshua, remained by Moses' side. After 40 days on the mountain with God, Moses and Joshua descended and returned to Aaron and the Israelites only to find that they had already betrayed their allegiance to God's commands by constructing the golden calf as an idol to worship.

> When Joshua heard the sound of the people as they shouted, he said to Moses, "There is a sound of war in the camp."
>
> But Moses replied:
> It's not the sound of a victory cry
> and not the sound of a cry of defeat;

> I hear the sound of singing!
> Exodus 32:17-18 (HCSB)

When the Psalmist (most likely King David) recalled this story, he cuts right to the heart of the matter:

> **Our fathers in Egypt did not grasp the significance of Your wonderful works or remember Your many acts of faithful love;**
>
> At Horeb they made a calf
> and worshiped the cast metal image.
> They exchanged their glory
> for the image of a grass-eating ox.
> Psalm 106: 7, 19-20 (HCSB)

For all God's displays of majesty and power, the Israelites never understood the significance of His works, the acts that pointed to His faithful love. Again and again, God showed faithful mercy to Israel. Again and again He revealed Himself to Aaron, but Aaron traded God's glory for what he could fashion and control with his own hands.

When God's love and faithfulness isn't at the heart of our worldview and theology, we will always end up trading His glory for a cheap imitation. When we rebuff God's invitation to come close and hear His voice, we will inevitably forget His instructions and miss out on the opportunity to encounter His majestic presence. When we substitute the raw, fiery power of God with something we can create and control ourselves, we always end up bowing down and singing praises to an idol.

The story of Israel in the wilderness is a frustrating, repeating pattern. God would display wonders of mercy and kindness. Israel would forget His love, complain, and violate God's holiness, thereby subjecting themselves to perilous judgement and wrath. Rinse and repeat for 40 years... Somewhere in this vicious cycle of discord, the Israelites seemed to forget the entire purpose for their time in the wilderness in the first place. Recall what Moses initially said to Pharaoh before Israel was free:

> Later, Moses and Aaron went in and said to Pharaoh, "This is what Yahweh, the God of Israel, says: Let My people go, so that they may hold a festival for Me in the wilderness."
> Exodus 5:1 (HCSB)

A journey through the wilderness is never supposed to be about wrath and judgement but is always intended to be an opportunity to worship God. The wilderness is a chance to meet God face to face, drink of His glory, and be equipped for what's in store in the Promised Land. The wilderness is all about worship.

This past weekend, Hannah and I said goodbye to our precious border collie/German shepherd mix Esther. I got Esther eight years ago when I desperately needed a friend, and she was that and so much more. She was one of the smartest, kindest, and happiest animals I have ever been around. Because Hannah and I both work from home when we're not traveling, Esther was a part of nearly every routine of the day. Two weeks ago, Hannah and I grew concerned because Esther's bright and energetic personality changed overnight. Our normally cheerful friend was sad and subdued. On Wednesday, after a week and a half of ups and downs, we took her to the vet, but the vet was unable to find any physical symptoms. He checked her thoroughly, and all her vitals were strong, her eyes were clear, and she didn't appear to be in any danger. So we went home with a mild pain medication, thinking perhaps she was sore from tweaking a muscle in her back or hips.

Thursday evening, we attended a connect group from our church, and when we arrived home, Esther hadn't moved from the spot where she was when we left, and she could barely walk when I let her outside. We planned to take her back to the vet first thing in the morning, and I spent much of the night sleeping next to her on the floor. Around 3:30am, she had a massive seizure. Later, the vet told me most dog seizures last 20-30 seconds, but this lasted 3-4 minutes, the most intense physical exertion I had ever seen this athletic dog ever have. I thought that at any moment that her heart might stop. As soon as it was over, we rushed her to the emergency veterinary clinic, and the staff told us she most likely had an aggressive brain tumor. Best case scenario, they said, we were merely buying time before she had another seizure, likely even worse than the first. With the rapid onset of her symptoms, our options were very limited, and we decided to take her home and spend our last day with her here.

Hannah and I made Esther as comfortable as we could, despite the fact that she was in great distress after the seizure. She paced frantically, stumbling with nearly every step, until she was too exhausted to stand any longer. Then she slept for several hours until she was strong enough to repeat the process. We loved her as best we knew how and took her on as many walks and as many trips outside as she wanted to go on, helping her stand upright, going as slow as she needed to go. We petted her and hugged her as many times as the day allowed, and we fed her all her favorite things for dinner: strawberries, ham, peanut butter, and Cheeze-Its. Esther died very quietly as the sun was setting.

The last three days have been some of the most painful and empty Hannah and I have spent together. Our eyes are sore and our bodies are exhausted from crying. Our house is dreadfully quiet, and everywhere we turn, in every space of our home, there are memories of our friend. Our hearts are smashed.

Esther was my first dog, and in eight years with her, I experienced so much of God's love, joy, and presence. Our walks around the neighborhood were always prime time for God to speak to me. So many of my testimonies feature Esther in a supporting role at some point in the story (some of these, you've read in this book). The emotions and attachment that we feel towards animals are God-given. When the prophet Nathan rebuked King David in 2 Samuel 12, he used the love of a pet to pull David's heart strings. David's son Solomon wrote in Proverbs 12 that how we care for our animals is a measure of righteousness. That bond is a powerful thing, and it's a reflection of God's heart for His creation.

Sunday morning, Hannah and I led worship for a congregation just outside of Nashville, and it was excruciating. We did our very best to pour out to God what He is worthy of, even though our hearts are so full of questions. In the evening, I was scheduled to volunteer for the very first time with the middle school students at our home church The Belonging Co.. I told Hannah that I wanted to follow through with serving, but I was nervous about the first part of the worship service because our church usually begins every gathering with joyful celebration. There is typically a lot of dancing and a lot of joyful shouting, neither of which were things I felt able to do. Upon arrival, the youth leader announced that the message of the day was "Praise is a Weapon," and we were going to lead the students in a big dance-praise party at the end of the service. Had I known beforehand, I probably wouldn't have shown up.

But I danced. And I praised. And I worshiped, giving God everything I knew how to give Him. Truthfully, it seemed dishonest and insincere to lead in something I felt like I had no business doing, but I was mindful of an old saying: "Feelings make excellent servants but terrible masters." I thought of King Jehoshaphat's armies who put their worshippers on the front lines (2 Chronicles 20). Surely they also felt insincere and dishonest. How could they have known the battle that God was fighting on their behalf when they were participating in something that seemed like madness at best and suicide at worst? Yet they worshiped, and we have their testimony to gain from.

It has been a very long time since I worshiped God without feeling His presence. Most of the time, it's easy to see that the economics of worship work entirely in our favor because we gain so much more from God's presence than we could ever bring to Him. Right now, however, worship feels costly for me and Hannah, and I am reminded that King David said, "I will not give a burnt offering that cost me nothing" (2 Samuel 24:24). We are giving everything we know how to give, doing our best to whole-heartedly and beautifully finish the tasks that God has assigned us. Hannah continues to paint and prepare a collection of artwork that will be on display this weekend, and I am continuing to sing and to write.

> For I consider that the sufferings of this present time are not worth comparing with the glory that is going to be revealed to us. For the creation eagerly waits with anticipation for God's sons to be revealed. For the creation was subjected to futility—not willingly, but because of Him who subjected it—in the hope that the creation itself will also be set free from the bondage of corruption into the glorious freedom of God's children. For we know that the whole creation has been groaning together with labor pains until now. And not only that, but we ourselves who have the Spirit as the first fruits—we also groan within ourselves, eagerly waiting for adoption, the redemption of our bodies.
> Romans 8:18-23 (HCSB)

At the end of the day, I know that we are rapidly headed towards a day when perfect is coming and we will know fully (1 Corinthians 13:12). Right now, however, I have more questions than I have answers, but I refuse to let my questions compromise that Truth that God has implanted in my heart. We have just a small window of opportunity to give God something now that we will never have the opportunity to give in Heaven: worship in the middle of pain, in the middle of questions, through loss, through not knowing, and through lack. So, that's what we're doing, praying that our worship rises before God as something sweet, even though in the moment it feels so bitter.

Neglecting worship during a season of difficulty hardens our hearts and leads our lips to complaints instead of praise.

Complaints, in turn, always take our eyes off the Lord and fix them instead on present circumstances. Complaining grinds faith down into frustration and fear.

We see in Numbers 13 that complaints and fear cost an entire generation of Israelites the opportunity to enter the Promised Land. After 40 days of spying out the land of Canaan, Israel rejected God's command to go in and occupy the land. They did so because 10 out of 12 spies lost sight of the beauty of God's promise and instead complained about the difficulties that lay ahead. The Israelites had not used their wilderness experience to equip themselves for the battles necessary to occupy the Promised Land and decided instead to disobey God's command to advance. The result of their disobedience was one year in the wilderness for every day the spies spent in Canaan.

During those 40 years, every single Israelite who was alive during the great Exodus from Egypt died. Even Moses eventually succumbed to the constant griping and squandered his chance to enter the Promised Land by disobeying God's command to speak to the rock, striking the rock in frustration instead. Only Joshua and Caleb (the two faithful spies) survived to enter the land along with the new generation of Israelites.

So what was the difference between Joshua's wilderness experience and everyone else's? How was Joshua able to maintain faith in God's promises when everyone else's faith crumbled? I think we find the answer by observing what Joshua was doing while everyone else was complaining. When everyone else refused to listen to God's voice, Joshua ascended Mt. Sinai with Moses and was present for the entire 40 days and nights in God's presence. There doesn't appear in Scripture any special invitation for Joshua to do so, but he latched onto God's initial invitation and did not let go. Joshua was hungry for God's voice.

Later, after the golden calf was destroyed, Moses set up the Tent of Meeting, where "anyone who wanted to consult with the Lord" could go and do so (Exodus 33:7); but once again, we see no one taking God up on the offer to meet with them. Instead, the entire congregation would stand outside their tents and watch as Moses went to the Tent of Meeting, and there he would speak to God. Everyone, that is, except for Joshua:

> As all the people saw the pillar of cloud remaining at the entrance to the tent, they would stand up, then bow in worship, each one at the door of his tent. The Lord spoke with Moses face to face, just as a man speaks with his friend. Then Moses would return to the camp, **but his assistant, the young man Joshua son of Nun, would not leave the inside of the tent.**
> Exodus 33:10-11 (HCSB)

Do you see the pattern of behavior? While everyone else refused to hear the voice of God for themselves, Joshua went and heard all of the commandments with his own ears. While everyone else stayed at the entrance to his tent, Joshua went with Moses to the tent of meeting. Even when Moses returned to the camp, Joshua stayed behind and would not leave the tent where God's presence was. **Joshua filled his ears with the voice of God and allowed God's presence to shape his faith.** He declined to participate in the complaining and fear, remaining faithful to God's command to possess the Promised Land when everyone else failed.

Which voices have you tuned your heart to, the voice of the crowd or the voice of the Lord? The crowd's voice leads to extra laps around the wilderness, while the Lord's voice leads to the fulfillment of Heaven's promises. Take a look back at how sin entered the world in the Garden of Eden. What was the first question God asked Adam after he admitted that he hid because he was ashamed of his nakedness?

> And he said, "I heard You in the garden and I was afraid because I was naked, so I hid."
> Then He asked, "Who told you that you were

> naked? Did you eat from the tree that I commanded you not to eat from?"
> Genesis 3:10-11 (HCSB)

God didn't say, "How could you do such a thing?" or "Shame on you! You had one job!" No. He asked Adam, "Who told you you were naked?" What voices have you been listening to? Instead of dwelling on the voice of the Lord, which Adam had access to every day, he turned to another voice, a voice that questioned the goodness at the core of God's nature.

This is exactly what happened in the wilderness during Israel's exodus. The people turned away from the voice of God and rejected the opportunity to echo His voice in worship. Instead, they listened to the voice of Satan, the accuser, that questioned God's loving kindness, and they partnered with it through their own complaints and accusations.

It's telling that during Joshua's first major test after entering the land of Canaan, when the Israelites arrived at the fortified city of Jericho, he gave the people a very particular strategic order:

> But Joshua had commanded the people: "Do not shout or let your voice be heard. Don't let one word come out of your mouth until the time I say, 'Shout!' Then you are to shout."
> Joshua 6:10 (HCSB)

I think you might call this "lesson learned." Having endured the Israelites' complaining for 40 years, seeing how it eroded their faith and cost an entire generation their opportunity to enter Canaan, Joshua didn't even give the people a chance to make that mistake again. When it's time to shout, we shout…until then, just shut up.

We see throughout the rest of Joshua's story a radical devotion to obedience of God's Word. For as long as he lived, Israel remained faithful to God's commandments. He relied on God for strategy and miraculous provision. He trusted God for discernment whenever the nation encountered problems. These were lessons he learned well during his 40 years in the wilderness, and all of them point back to his hunger for God's voice. God used Joshua's hunger in the wilderness to qualify him for leadership in the Promised Land.

We started in Chapter 1 of this book with a passage from Psalm 95 that Christ Church in my home town of Nashville, Tennessee recites nearly every Sunday:

> Come, let us sing to the lord!
> Let us shout joyfully to the Rock of our salvation.
> Let us come to him with thanksgiving.
> Let us sing psalms of praise to him.
> For the lord is a great God,
> a great King above all gods.
> He holds in his hands the depths of the earth
> and the mightiest mountains.
> The sea belongs to him, for he made it.
> His hands formed the dry land, too.
> Come, let us worship and bow down.
> Let us kneel before the lord our maker,
> for he is our God.
> We are the people he watches over,
> the flock under his care.
> **If only you would listen to his voice today!**
> Psalm 95:1-8 (NLT)

That's verses 1-8, but here's the rest. Look at the context of that last sentence:

> **If only you would listen to his voice today!**
> **The Lord says, "Don't harden your hearts as Israel did at Meribah, as they did at Massah in the wilderness.**

> For there your ancestors tested and tried my
> patience,
> even though they saw everything I did.
> For forty years I was angry with them, and I said,
> 'They are a people whose hearts turn away from
> me.
> They refuse to do what I tell them.'
> So in my anger I took an oath:
> 'They will never enter my place of rest.'"
> Psalm 95:8-11 (NLT)

Meribah is the place where Moses struck the rock instead of listening to God's instruction to speak to the rock. Meribah is where Moses joined Israel in rejecting the Voice. Following the Voice is the key to entering God's promised place of rest. If only you would listen to His voice today!

It's human nature to want to avoid the wilderness. After all, the wilderness is usually difficult and puts us face to face with our fears. **But it's vital to realize that not only does God use the wilderness, He ordains it.** It's part of His design to shape our character and qualify us for our lives of worship. He doesn't send us there to fail! Oftentimes, we resist the harsh landscape of the wilderness, much like the children of Israel did when they called it an "evil place," not realizing that it was God who sent us there with a divine purpose.

To understand this principle, let's look at Jesus' season in the wilderness. When Jesus was baptized by John, the heavens were ripped open and the Holy Spirit descended upon Him in the form of a dove (Mark 1:9-11). Look what happened next:

> As soon as He came up out of the water, He saw
> the heavens being torn open and the Spirit
> descending to Him like a dove. And a voice came
> from heaven:
>
> You are My beloved Son;
> I take delight in You!

Immediately the Spirit drove Him into the wilderness.
Mark 1:10-12 (HCSB)

The Holy Spirit's first mission objective for Jesus was the wilderness. The other Gospel accounts affirm this. Both Matthew's and Luke's accounts actually say that the Holy Spirit drove Jesus into the wilderness *to be tempted* by the Devil.

Now, let's not make a mistake here and think that God the Father dangled the temptation of sin in front of Jesus as a test to see if He might stumble. In the same way, when God ordains a season in the wilderness, and we face temptation there, we can be confident that God is not the one tempting us to sin.

> No one undergoing a trial should say, "I am being tempted by God." For God is not tempted by evil, and He Himself doesn't tempt anyone.
> James 1:13 (HCSB)

God will never set you up to fail. There's something else going on here, and it's important we don't miss it. The Holy Spirit did not drive Jesus into the wilderness to be tempted by Satan with the possible outcome of defeat. No! He drove Jesus into the wilderness with the objective of unquestionable, crushing victory over Satan and sin.

Just like we observed Joshua, let's look at how Jesus achieved victory in the wilderness. The first thing we see is that Jesus fasted for 40 days and 40 nights (Matthew 4:2), the same as Moses did on the mountain. This rendered His flesh weak, but the Holy Spirit within Him was strong (Matthew 26:41).

As Christians, fasting is one of the best available tools to tune our hearts to the voice of God. If the voice of God is like a radio signal, our flesh is like a giant white noise maker! Nothing tunes our hearts to God's frequency like denying our flesh what it wants (food, social media, TV, movies, etc). Jesus modeled this principle for us on multiple occasions. We would be wise to make it a regular part of our Christian walk, constantly putting to death the flesh and fine-tuning our spiritual antennae to hear God's voice more clearly. It's somewhat counterintuitive, but the moment Jesus' body was at its weakest was precisely when He was best equipped to face Satan's temptation.

Not surprisingly, Jesus' bodily weakness was the first place Satan tempted Him.

> After He had fasted 40 days and 40 nights, He was hungry. Then the tempter approached Him and said, "If You are the Son of God, tell these stones to become bread."
>
> But He answered, "It is written: Man must not live on bread alone but on every word that comes from the mouth of God."
> Matthew 4:2-4 (HCSB)

Satan tempted Jesus in three main areas in which all Christians are tested. **First he challenged Jesus' identity: "If you are the Son of God…"** Satan knew that if he could compromise Jesus' identity, He might fall prey to the temptation to prove Himself. It's the same way a schoolyard bully taunts: prove you're not a wimp by taking a swing at me!

But Jesus was fully confident in the Father's voice He heard at His baptism that said, "This is my beloved Son, with whom I am well pleased" (Matthew 3:17). Like Joshua, Jesus clung to the truth of God's voice and did not let go. There was no doubt in Him that caused insecurity or any need to prove Himself because He was confident in the identity that God declared over Him.

Likewise, Satan will always challenge the identity that God pronounced over us. As Christians, we bear the identity of Christ's righteousness (2 Corinthians 5:21). Satan always challenges us by calling into question what God has spoken.

When he tempted Eve in the Garden of Eden, he started by questioning what God's voice had spoken to her: "Did God really say you must not eat the fruit from any of the trees in the garden?" (Genesis 3:1) This is why I started this book by diving into our identity, the new name God gave to us, just like Jacob named the place where God met him Bethel. **When we are in Christ, Satan has no power to compromise our identity: he can only cause us to question it.**

> Then the Devil took Him to the holy city, had Him stand on the pinnacle of the temple, and said to Him, "If You are the Son of God, throw Yourself down. For it is written:
>
> He will give His angels orders concerning you, and they will support you with their hands so that you will not strike your foot against a stone."
>
> Jesus told him, "It is also written: Do not test the Lord your God."
> Matthew 4:5-7 (HCSB)

Next, Satan attacked the promises God made to Jesus in this life. Essentially, what the Devil was doing was calling into question God's goodness. Does He really care about you enough to make good on all these promises? Shouldn't you test it out before you really trust Him? Satan tempted Jesus to make the same mistake that Moses and the Israelites made in the wilderness: to question God's loving nature. It's the same tactic he used on Eve to cause her to take her eyes off God's goodness: "In fact, God knows that when you eat it your eyes will be opened and you will be like God, knowing good and evil" (Genesis 3:5). In other words, Satan lied to her saying, "God's not really all you think He is. He's holding out on you!"

It's interesting that with Jesus, the Devil actually used a quote from Scripture to do his tempting. The particular passage he quoted here is from Psalm 91:11-12, but Satan showed his cards by leaving out the next two verses:

> You will tread on the lion and the cobra;
> you will trample the young lion and the serpent.
> Because he is lovingly devoted to Me,
> I will deliver him;
> I will protect him because he knows My name.
> Psalm 91:13-14

It's just like Satan to dangle a partial promise in front of us to tempt us into shortcutting our way into God's blessings. But when we are lovingly devoted to Him, He will always deliver us. When we know His name, and we're confident in His loving nature, we are protected from Satan's distortions and half truths. In John 17:26, Jesus said that He makes God's name known to all His disciples so that we would receive the same love the Father gave to the Son. **When we are in Christ, Satan has no power to compromise God's promises; he can only cause us to question God's nature.**

> Again, the Devil took Him to a very high mountain and showed Him all the kingdoms of the world and their splendor. And he said to Him, "I will give You all these things if You will fall down and worship me."
>
> Then Jesus told him, "Go away, Satan! For it is written:
> Worship the Lord your God,
> and serve only Him."
>
> Then the Devil left Him, and immediately angels came and began to serve Him.
> Matthew 4:8-11 (HCSB)

Lastly, Satan attacked Jesus' destiny. Satan knew that Jesus was sent from Heaven to bring the Kingdom of God here to earth. He offered Jesus a short cut, and he did it by tempting Jesus away from true worship. Satan often exploits the calling of God on our lives as an opportunity to sabotage our true created purpose, which is to worship God. The Israelites entered the wilderness with the promise of Canaan before them, but Satan lured them astray by tempting them to worship the golden calf, that which they'd made with their own hands. However, Joshua kept the true splendor of God before his face and did not fall prey to worshiping cheap imitations.

Similarly, Jacob was born with the promise that God would bless him as a great nation (Genesis 25:23), and God reaffirmed that promise to him at Bethel. But Jacob persisted in attempting to short-cut and manipulate his way into that destiny. It's sometimes easy to excuse sin with the notion that compromise puts us closer to the our God-given destiny. However, no reward Satan dangles in front of us could ever come close to equaling the fullness of God's promises. The purpose of any calling God has given you ultimately is to glorify Him, and any short cut the Devil offers is simply a lie. **Satan has no power to compromise or fulfill your destiny; he can only tempt you to sell yourself short by redirecting your worship away from God.**

Jesus' 40 days in the wilderness was an unequivocal dismantling of Satan's lies. He clearly demonstrated how little power Satan actually has by living out what is later articulated in James 4:7: "Submit to God, but resist the Devil and he will flee from you." Satan's authority over your life was crushed the moment you submitted your life to Jesus.

Luke's gospel tells us that when Jesus left the wilderness, He "returned to Galilee in the power of the Spirit" (Luke 4:14). The same Holy Spirit that descended on Him at His baptism drove Him into the wilderness to be tempted; and after He defeated Satan, Jesus began His ministry in power! The wilderness test that the Spirit led Christ through qualified and equipped Him to do what the Father sent Him to do.

In the same way, don't resist the wilderness seasons the Holy Spirit leads you into. Instead, take the opportunity to worship God in the barren place and tune your heart to His voice. Cling to God's Word, to the new identity He spoke over you at the cross, to the truth of His loving nature, and your created purpose to bring glory to Him alone. When temptation comes, remember that God is not setting you up for failure but leading you into total victory over the schemes of Satan. Know that in the wilderness, God is equipping you to accomplish all that He has called you to in the power of the Holy Spirit!

Throughout this life of worship, as we step further and further into God's purposes and calling, we may enter many wilderness seasons. As we scale mountaintops and traverse valleys, it's important that we learn how to remain rooted in God's truth, tuned to His voice and not the lies of the enemy. The good news is that because of Christ, we will always enter the wilderness with the same Holy Spirit that rested on Jesus and empowered His victory over sin and death (Romans 8:11)!

Just as Satan did with the Israelites and with Jesus, he will often try to call into question the fundamental truths of our faith. One of his many tactics is to use present circumstances to call into question God's nature or our identity in Him. Our experiences or circumstances can sometimes be so profoundly difficult that we find ourselves questioning things we once knew beyond a shadow of doubt.

John the Baptist was in prison when he sent his two disciples to ask Jesus if he had made a mistake in proclaiming that Jesus was the Messiah. As the son of Zachariah the priest, it is highly likely that John was aware of the Messiah's job description from Isaiah's prophecy:

> The Spirit of the Lord God is on Me,
> because the Lord has anointed Me
> to bring good news to the poor.
> He has sent Me to heal the brokenhearted,
> to proclaim liberty to the captives
> and freedom to the prisoners;
> Isaiah 61:1 (HCSB)

However, John found himself in prison after heralding the

One who was supposed to proclaim freedom to the prisoners. Something didn't add up. But rather than allowing what he didn't understand to undermine his faith, he sent two of his disciples to ask Jesus if he had somehow gotten it wrong. It's important to note, however, that at the time of Jesus' baptism, John *knew that he knew* that Jesus was the Messiah because he saw the heavens rend and the Holy Spirit descend upon Jesus. He heard the thunderous voice from Heaven say, "This is my beloved son. I take delight in Him!" (Matthew 3)

Rotting in prison, however, John had understandable questions that challenged the validity of his revelation of Jesus, but he didn't allow those questions to compromise his faith. One of the biggest dangers we face as Christians is allowing our questions to undermine the Gospel that has been revealed to us. We allow what we see with our natural eyes, our doubts and our fears, to crumble our resolve to complete our assignment as disciples.

Not coincidentally, I believe, Isaiah 61 is the same passage that Jesus read aloud at the synagogue in Nazareth before the mob tried to throw Him off a cliff. The crowd there did what John the Baptist refused to do: they allowed their questions and what they saw with their natural eyes to erode the revelation of Jesus that was stirring in their hearts. John the Baptist and the congregation at Nazareth both had the same opportunity and challenge presented to them. Both had the choice between the revelation of Jesus and the questions that arose because of what they saw in the natural. The crowd chose to embrace their questions as reality, but John chose to take his questions to Jesus and allow allow Him to bolster his faith.

Many times, what's written in the Bible seems at odds with our experience, but that does not authorize us to change the assignment God has called us to. Our experiences (or lack thereof) don't excuse us from faithfully living out the commandments in God's Word, but often times, rather than being obedient, we actually come up with theologies that excuse our disobedience.

For the sake of example: in Mark 16 (and many other other passages in Scripture), Jesus says that believers will "lay hands on the sick and they will get well." One part of that is our assignment, and the other part is completely within God's power. Without God, I don't have the power to heal the common cold or a hangnail. But in Matthew 10, Jesus actually tells His disciples "heal the sick." My assignment is to lay hands on the sick and trust God to do what only He can do. But most of us have prayed for someone who was sick who didn't recover. What should we do with this apparent discrepancy between what is revealed to us in the Word and our lack of experience? We are not authorized to change the assignment. We are not authorized to come up with theological excuses for disobeying the command to heal the sick. Like John the Baptist in prison (despite Isaiah's prophecy that the Messiah would free the prisoner), we must remain faithful to the assignment given to us.

This is what I believe God was saying to me years ago when He told me, "I don't need a new PR person; I just need someone who will obey." Since that day, I have watched hundreds of people I prayed for be dramatically and miraculously healed, often instantaneously! However, I have also prayed for many people who did not get healed. Do I fully understand it? No. But I refuse to create a theology based on my unanswered questions rather than the Truth in God's Word. I will continue praying for the sick because that is the commandment Jesus gave to His disciples. I will celebrate the victories, but I will not give my defeats the power to compromise my faith. And when my heart begins to doubt because something in my experience doesn't line up with what I read in the Bible, I will get alone with God and ask Him to show me what to do. That's what the disciples did when they prayed for the boy who didn't receive deliverance (Matthew 17). They approached Jesus in private and asked Him what went wrong. Jesus showed them both the symptom (lack of faith) and the solution for that particular case (prayer and fasting).

I have used the example of praying for the sick, but this principle applies broadly to all our areas of doubt. Even when we don't see people coming to Christ, we're not excused from the commission to preach the Gospel. When what we see around us is poverty, we're not excused from gratitude for God's blessings. When we don't experience breakthrough, we're not excused from trusting God to supply all our needs.

Don't be discouraged when you are plagued by questions. Don't give up on your assignment. Don't embrace theologies that excuse you from obedience to God's Word. **Doubt is always an invitation to go spend time alone with Jesus.** Surrender your burdens and questions to Him, and allow Him to change your perspective. He is the author and the perfecter of our faith (Hebrews 12:2).

One day, when we are in Heaven, we will see Jesus in the fullness of His glory. In that place, surrounded by His perfect light that casts no shadow, there will be no more tears of sorrow. There will be no more sin, pain, destruction, or poverty. Confusion will cease because we will see Him as He truly is. Sickness and suffering will be eradicated from existence. On that day, we will worship Him in uncompromised fullness of joy. But for now, we have the opportunity to embrace Him in our pain and sorrow, knowing that this is a love offering we will no longer be able to give Him in Heaven.

The joy will come. God will lead you out of the wilderness if you continue pursuing Him. But don't wait to worship Him. Worshiping Jesus in the midst of brokenness is a holy sacrifice that is only available in this one brief lifetime. Don't let the opportunity pass you by.

There have been seasons in my life where I felt strange kinship to the children of Israel in their 40 years of wandering. On more than one occasion, I found myself taking yet another lap around the same wilderness, recognizing that I was being presented with the same tests over and over again. Do I really trust God in my relationships? Do I really trust Him in my finances? Have I really surrendered my career to Him? Have I really learned to obey His voice even when it doesn't make sense? Occasionally, I find myself failing the same tests multiple times, but God refuses to allow me to wallow in failure. He simply takes me by the hand, lifts me up, and says, "Come with me. Let's try that again." God's mercies are new every morning. He is never content to leave us in defeat.

We can see this is true by observing the amazing number of parallels between the Israelites' 40 wilderness years and Jesus' 40 wilderness days. Israel passed through the waters of the Red Sea before God led them through the wilderness. Jesus passed through the waters of baptism before the Holy Spirit also led Him into the very same wilderness.

Where Israel found themselves without food or water and failed to have faith, Jesus trusted wholly in God's power and successfully passed that test. When Israel saw the Promised Land, they failed to trust that God would deliver to them that kingdom, but when Satan showed Jesus the very same Promised Land, He passed the test and trusted that His victory would come from the Father. Where Israel bowed down to a false idol, Jesus refused to bow down to Satan.

What's more, where Israel failed to listen to the voice of God, Jesus relied upon the same voice to rebuke Satan during His temptation. Every verse that Jesus quoted to Satan during His temptation was from Moses' farewell address to Israel in Deuteronomy chapters 6-8. This is one of the most important passages in the Torah, and Moses actually begins by saying:

> "Listen, Israel: The Lord our God, the Lord is One. Love the Lord your God with all your heart, with all your soul, and with all your strength. These words that I am giving you today are to be in your heart. Repeat them to your children. Talk about them when you sit in your house and when you walk along the road, when you lie down and when you get up. Bind them as a sign on your hand and let them be a symbol on your forehead. Write them on the doorposts of your house and on your gates.
> Deuteronomy 6:4-9 (HCSB)

Jesus applied the lessons of Israel's wilderness years, the words that God spoke that Israel refused to listen to; and in 40 days, He accomplished what Israel could not do in 40 years. Then, at the cross, Jesus finished what He started in the wilderness, delivering the final and fatal blow to sin's power over God's people. Because of the cross, Jesus' victory in the wilderness is now our own!

We are not doomed to repeat the devastating failures of Israel. We are not powerless to resist Satan's temptation. We have been given ears to hear God's voice and power by the Holy Spirit to obey and live righteously! We are no longer defined by our stumbles and missteps but by the triumph of Jesus.

Take a look at how the author of Hebrews records Moses' story:

> By faith Moses, when he had grown up, refused to be called the son of Pharaoh's daughter and chose to suffer with the people of God rather than to enjoy the short-lived pleasure of sin. For he considered the reproach because of the Messiah to be greater wealth than the treasures of Egypt, since his attention was on the reward.
>
> By faith he left Egypt behind, not being afraid of the king's anger, for Moses persevered as one who sees Him who is invisible. By faith he instituted the Passover and the sprinkling of the blood, so that the destroyer of the firstborn might not touch the Israelites. By faith they crossed the Red Sea as though they were on dry land. When the Egyptians attempted to do this, they were drowned.
>
> By faith the walls of Jericho fell down after being encircled by the Israelites for seven days.
> Hebrews 11:24-30 (HCSB)

What's missing from this account? Any whiff of Moses' failure! Similarly, Hebrews 11 records that Abraham and Sarah received their promised son Isaac by unwavering faith, despite the fact that Sarah laughed in unbelief and Abraham doubted so much that he slept with Sarah's concubine and fathered Ishmael. Chapter 6 of Hebrews states that Abraham "waited patiently and obtained the promise." Gideon is recorded as a man of great faith despite his idolatry. Sampson is recorded as a man of great faith despite his violation of the Nazirite vow and sin with Delilah. David is recorded as a hero of the faith and in Acts 13:22 is regarded as "a man after God's own heart" despite his adultery and murder. What's going on here?

In chapter 8 of Hebrews, the author quotes the Old Testament prophet Jeremiah:

> "Look, the days are coming" — this is the Lord's declaration — "when I will make a new covenant with the house of Israel and with the house of Judah. This one will not be like the covenant I made with their ancestors when I took them by the hand to bring them out of the land of Egypt — a covenant they broke even though I had married them" — the Lord's declaration. "Instead, this is the covenant I will make with the house of Israel after those days" — the Lord's declaration. "I will put My teaching within them and write it on their hearts. I will be their God, and they will be My people. No longer will one teach his neighbor or his brother, saying, 'Know the Lord,' for they will all know Me, from the least to the greatest of them" — this is the Lord's declaration. **"For I will forgive their wrongdoing and never again remember their sin.**
> Jeremiah 31:31-34 (HCSB)

Jesus is the fulfillment of this prophecy. Because of His victory, our stories pass through the cross clean of the tarnish of sin. When we are in Christ, God rewrites our history free of blemish. He who remembers the number of hairs on each of our heads actually chooses to forget our rebellion, recalling only the perfection of His beloved Son.

We, just like Jesus, now have the teachings of God written upon our hearts by the Holy Spirit. We are ready and empowered to resist and repel the temptations of the enemy. And even when we fall short, our victory remains, not in our own steadfastness but in His. Truly, the wilderness is no longer Satan's territory but a sanctuary in which God's people worship Him for who He is and all He has done!

12 MAKE DISCIPLES

The altar of your life has a dual purpose. As we have explored and pondered throughout this book, we are walking, talking sanctuaries of worship, ambassadors of the culture of Heaven. We are living sacrifices, freewill offerings of adoration to the God who loved us first, with every aspect of our being consecrated to the glory of Him. But God did not call us into consecration simply for our own sake. Just like the altars of the Old Testament, our lives serve as monuments to the world around us that God showed up and changed everything!

After Moses died, God called Joshua to consecrate the people of Israel and prepare them to enter the Promised Land. Just as God does so often throughout Scripture, He gave a tremendous sign to Joshua and the Israelites that reflected what He'd already done for them once before. For Moses and the previous generation, God parted the Red Sea and allowed them to walk across on dry land, but Joshua and Caleb were the only two adults still alive to remember what God had done. So, for a new generation, God demonstrated once again that He was with them by holding back the raging waters of the Jordan River and allowing Israel to walk across on dry land. This time, God instructed Joshua to build an altar that would serve as a monument for future generations of God's presence and provision:

> After the entire nation had finished crossing the Jordan, the Lord spoke to Joshua: "Choose 12 men from the people, one man for each tribe, and command them: Take 12 stones from this place in the middle of the Jordan where the priests are standing, carry them with you, and set them down at the place where you spend the night."
>
> So Joshua summoned the 12 men he had selected from the Israelites, one man for each tribe, and said to them, "Go across to the ark of the Lord your God in the middle of the Jordan. Each of you lift a stone onto his shoulder, one for each of the Israelite tribes, so that this will be a sign among you. **In the future, when your children ask you, 'What do these stones mean to you?' you should tell them, 'The waters of the Jordan were cut off in front of the ark of the Lord's covenant. When it crossed the Jordan, the Jordan's waters were cut off.' Therefore these stones will always be a memorial for the Israelites."**
>
> Joshua 4:1-9 (HCSB)

There are two important aspects of Joshua's altar that we can apply to our own lives. First, we should live in such a way that leads people to ask, "What took place here?" Second, we should be prepared to give them an answer, a testimony of exactly what God has done.

Ultimately, every disciple of Jesus has the same testimony: we were far from God and He came near! We were once outside and were welcomed in. We were lost and are now found. We were blind, but now we see! However, God fills in all the details in each of our stories in beautiful colors and tones, and these display some aspect of His character that we are uniquely qualified to highlight. My story looks a little different than yours, and yours looks a little different than the next person's; thus God has written details into each of His children's stories that must all be told so that the world sees a more complete image of His glory. Heaven is a kaleidoscope of redeemed humanity!

Your story is important, even if you feel like it's not. You might not think that your testimony carries any weight or importance, but God chose you for a reason. There's a reason He didn't beam you straight up to Heaven the moment you gave your life to Christ. He left you here, an ambassador of Heaven in a land that is no longer your true home, so that you can be salt and light. Your light is important, for it casts a distinct glow of God's glory onto people and places that no once else is able to illuminate in the same way.

Sometimes, I think about the Body of Christ (the Church of which all disciples of Jesus are members) as a massive stained glass window. Each of us is an individual piece of colored glass. Our shapes are not uniform. In fact, if you examine each one of us in isolation, it would appear that we are broken, with jagged edges and undefined shapes. However, each piece of glass has its own unique beauty, and when God's light shines through us we glow with brilliant color. There are more colors, shapes, and sizes in this vast mosaic of light than you could ever imagine!

When you step back and look at the window as a whole, you will find a whole other level of beauty on display. Each piece of glass fills in a portion of the picture, and what gets illuminated when you see them all together is the matchless beauty of Jesus! God the Father chose you, gave you your individual shape and color, illuminated your life through the Holy Spirit, and placed you perfectly in space and time to declare to the world the splendor of His Son!

What's more, God has commissioned you to go into the world and tell others that they too have a unique and beautiful place in this incredible image. What qualifies us for this work is simply that we spend time in the presence of Jesus. Early on in the book of Acts, the Apostle Peter (remember, the one who, just a few chapters earlier, denied Jesus) preached before the same Sanhedrin that put Jesus on trial. Following the example of Jesus, Peter had lifted up the lame man lying at the gate of the temple and then preached the Gospel to those gathered at the temple. A healing always makes for a fantastic sermon illustration! Look at what the leaders of the Sanhedrin observed about Peter:

> When they observed the boldness of Peter and John and realized that they were uneducated and untrained men, they were amazed and recognized that they had been with Jesus. And since they saw the man who had been healed standing with them, they had nothing to say in response.
> Acts 4:13-14 (HCSB)

They saw that Peter had been *with* Jesus. Being with Jesus qualified this uneducated fisherman to preach the Gospel with such boldness that the Sanhedrin were unable to bring accusations against him. Having followed and observed Jesus' ways, having been transformed by Him, Peter now went about doing the same work that Jesus began. This is the commission of every disciple:

> Then Jesus came near and said to them, "All authority has been given to Me in heaven and on earth. **Go, therefore, and make disciples** of all nations, baptizing them in the name of the Father and of the Son and of the Holy Spirit, teaching them to observe everything I have commanded you. And remember, I am with you always, to the end of the age."
> Matthew 28:18-20 (HCSB)

If we are not making disciples, we are fundamentally missing the mark of the Great Commission. You are called to take the Light of Christ wherever you go and shine it on everyone through your words and deeds so that they may also be lit aflame. As I have said before, this is not a commission only to pastors, missionaries, church workers, or evangelists. This is a command to every single disciple of Jesus. It doesn't require that you are the best or the brightest. It doesn't require that you have all the answers. It requires simply that you uncover the light already within you:

> "You are the light of the world. A city situated on a hill cannot be hidden. No one lights a lamp and puts it under a basket, but rather on a lampstand, and it gives light for all who are in the house. In the same way, let your light shine before men, so that they may see your good works and give glory to your Father in heaven.
> Matthew 5:14-16 (HCSB)

God did not illuminate your life only for you to keep His light to yourself. It is not His design for you to look around, compare your light to the color and brightness of what others have, and dismiss yourself because you don't seem to be as vibrant as somebody else.

I love this quote by A.W. Tozer, an American pastor and author from the mid 1900s:

"Others before me have gone much farther into these holy mysteries than I have done, but if my fire is not large it is yet real, and there may be those who can light their candle at its flame."[8]

No matter how small or dim your flame might appear to you, it is bright enough to light someone else's. All it takes is a spark!

It is no accident that we get to see such a quick turnaround in Peter's life. Only 4 chapters in the Bible separate the moment when Peter denied knowing Jesus in John 18 to when Peter led 3,000 people to Christ in Acts 2. Once your life has been marked by the presence of Jesus, it is the most natural thing in the world to share your faith with others.

Take a look at the story of someone who, by all outward appearances, should have been the *least* qualified person to be

---

[8] Tozer, A.W.. *The Pursuit of God.* Christian Publications. Harrisburg PA. 1948.

an evangelist for Jesus:

> When He got out on land, a demon-possessed man from the town met Him. For a long time he had worn no clothes and did not stay in a house but in the tombs. When he saw Jesus, he cried out, fell down before Him, and said in a loud voice, "What do You have to do with me, Jesus, You Son of the Most High God? I beg You, don't torment me!" For He had commanded the unclean spirit to come out of the man. Many times it had seized him, and though he was guarded, bound by chains and shackles, he would snap the restraints and be driven by the demon into deserted places.
>
> "What is your name?" Jesus asked him. "Legion," he said — because many demons had entered him. And they begged Him not to banish them to the abyss.
> Luke 8:27-31 (HCSB)

Here is a man from whom Satan had robbed every shred of identity, no longer able to wear clothes, no longer able to co-exist with society, living in a graveyard. Satan's lie to him was, "This is your neighborhood. You belong here with the dead. You have no name but that of the many demons inside of you." But something inside this man stirred when He saw Jesus arrive on the shores of his town. He caught a glimpse of a light more powerful than the darkness within him, and he ran and fell at Jesus' feet.

> A large herd of pigs was there, feeding on the hillside. The demons begged Him to permit them to enter the pigs, and He gave them permission. The demons came out of the man and entered the pigs, and the herd rushed down the steep bank into the lake and drowned. When the men who tended them saw what had happened, they ran off and reported it in the town and in the countryside. Then people

went out to see what had happened. They came to Jesus and found the man the demons had departed from, sitting at Jesus' feet, dressed and in his right mind. And they were afraid. Meanwhile, the eyewitnesses reported to them how the demon-possessed man was delivered. Then all the people of the Gerasene region asked Him to leave them, because they were gripped by great fear. So getting into the boat, He returned.

The man from whom the demons had departed kept begging Him to be with Him. **But He sent him away and said, "Go back to your home, and tell all that God has done for you." And off he went, proclaiming throughout the town all that Jesus had done for him.**
Luke 8:32-39 (HCSB)

Legion had a one-time encounter with Jesus. **One day in the presence of the Messiah qualified him to preach the Gospel to his neighbors.** Neither the years he spent living naked in the graveyard nor the many people he had hurt disqualified him.

Part of me wishes that we knew more of Legion's story. I wish we could know what his real name was before Satan destroyed his identity. I wish we could know what else Jesus said to him that day. But I suspect that the details are left out intentionally so that none of us would read his story and find reason to excuse ourselves from taking up the command to preach the Gospel. **One encounter with Jesus was all it took. How much more are we, who have both the Word and the Spirit, qualified to preach the same Gospel?**

When I was a young kid, whenever I reached the end of an epic novel or series like *Treasure Island*, *Lord of the Rings*, or *The Chronicles of Narnia*, something deep inside of me always groaned, yearning to live with that kind of purpose and adventure. I would read the last page and suddenly be filled with acute sadness that the adventure was over, and I had to return to my ordinary life. Looking back, I believe that what I felt was actually the Holy Spirit stirring a holy dissatisfaction with natural life, calling me into true, *super*-natural living.

You see, with Christ, our lives carry more purpose and importance than any work of fiction. I believe that the whole world is attracted to stories of adventure because God created each of us with an innate sense that we were designed for more than the ordinary. We are called to heal the sick and raise the dead to life! The Christian life is meant to be the grandest of all adventures, not a boring repetition of Sundays followed by six days that all look and feel the same. Now that we have encountered the Living God, we are commissioned to go and make more disciples. The first step is simply to go.

At the Last Supper, just before Jesus was crucified, He gave the disciples a new instruction that we are to carry with us until the end of time:

> "I give you a new command: Love one another. Just as I have loved you, you must also love one another. By this all people will know that you are My disciples, if you have love for one another."
> John 13:34-35 (HCSB)

I spent a long season of my life reading those verses over and over again, filled with a conviction that my love did not match the love that Jesus described here. My love tends to be moody and fickle. It often depends on whether or not I have had coffee that morning. My love has good days and bad days. What kind of love is so profound that that when the world observes how I treat those around me, they would say, "This person must be a disciple of Jesus"? What kind of love is it that causes someone outside the faith to stop and say, "There's something different going on here."?

Shortly after college, I spent nearly a year praying that God would teach me how to love the way He commanded His disciples. One weekend, I went on a retreat with young adults from my church. It was an emotional trip because one of our worship leaders had just been diagnosed with non-Hodgkin's lymphoma, an aggressive and deadly cancer. Her name was Sarah, and she had a 14-inch long tumor wrapped around her heart, literally choking the life out of her.

Sarah was scheduled to go in for her second chemotherapy treatment the week after the retreat. The second treatment is typically the one after which a patient's hair begins to fall out. Sarah couldn't bear the thought of losing her beautiful hair in clumps and handfuls. Wanting to get it over with, she asked one of the pastors from our church to take hair clippers and shave her head while we were on the retreat. So, we stood around Sarah, laid our hands on her, and prayed for God's healing touch in her body. Then we tearfully watched as our pastor shaved Sarah's head.

When it was finished, Sarah half-jokingly asked, "Does anybody else want to shave their head? We've got the clippers all ready for you!"

Immediately, I felt the Holy Spirit speak as clearly as I've ever heard Him: *"This is it! This is what you've been asking me for. This is the kind of love I was talking about in John 13."*

I raised my hand and said, "I'll do it!" And I asked Sarah if she would be the one to shave my head for me. At the time, I had long hair, and for some stupid reason, that was important to me. But in that moment, nothing was more important than walking beside my friend in solidarity as she battled cancer. We both laughed and cried as she took the clippers and shaved every strand of hair off my head. I told her that I would keep my head shaved until she was fully recovered.

That simple act of love provided me with more opportunities to share the Gospel with others than any other thing I've ever done. Over and over again, friends would be shocked to see me without hair and asked why I had shaved my head. My bank card had a photo on it of me with long hair, and every time I used it to pay for something, the person handling the transaction would do a double-take and ask me what happened to my hair. I would explain that I had shaved my head in solidarity with a friend who was undergoing chemo treatment.

Time and time again, people would say something that I never expected to hear that night Sarah shaved my head: "Wow! That's amazing! I don't know if I love anyone enough to do that." I used each opportunity to explain that love like that doesn't come from myself but from Jesus inside of me.

Today, ten years later, Sarah is fully recovered. She is married and the mother of two beautiful children, a walking testimony of Jesus' healing power. Her hair has grown back, and so has mine. But I will never be the same again.

The world recognizes and craves the love of Christ, even if they don't know how to identify it. Through simple acts of kindness and radical expressions of selfless love, we announce to those around us who we are and whose we are. We show them a culture that is not of this world. The way you love has the potential to change someone else's life.

We are called to lives of extravagant love and uncompromising obedience. As the Apostle Paul told the Church in Galatians 2:20, our lives are no longer our own but are laid down for the One who laid down His life for us. This grand adventure of faith, this sacred mission to make disciples of every nation on earth, will take you further than you've ever imagined possible so long as you give God a continual "yes" to what He asks of you. Don't worry about what your life looks like right now, for God will not waste a heart that is committed to obedience.

Moments will come when what God is calling you to will feel like a big risk. But rest assured, when you step out in faith, God will meet you there and show up in ways that only He can. My friend Bishop Dan Scott says, "You might not be able to part the Red Sea, but you can hold out your staff over the water. God will do the rest."

Jesus announced in John 8:12, "I am the light of the world." But before He ascended into Heaven, He passed the baton to His disciples, and told us, "You are the light of the world" (Matthew 5:14). We are actually called to do more than *reflect* God's light. We're called to *shine!*

> "Every generous act and every perfect gift is from above, coming down from the Father of lights; with Him there is no variation or shadow cast by turning."
> James 1:17 (HCSB)

The light that comes from God casts no shadow. Anything that merely reflects light always casts a shadow on the other side, and you can see that shadow change as the object turns: "the shadow cast by turning." But God's light doesn't do that. God's light actually transforms what it touches, so that it too begins to shine with the same light. That's why He is called the "Father of lights," because His children also glow with His light. We are called to burn with this transformative light so that our light might fall on others, and their lives might also be transformed from darkness into light.

Nobody is perfect at this. The Apostle Paul tells us in 1 Corinthians 13:12 that, right now, we still see imperfectly "as in a mirror," but we are in the process of being transformed, and we look forward to the day when we will see God's light perfectly. Revelation 21:23 tells us that in Heaven, God's light will be so completely revealed that there will no longer be a need for the sun and moon to shine! We eagerly anticipate that day, but let's not forget how Jesus taught us to pray: "on earth as it is in Heaven." We already have, by faith, access to behold the glory of God here and now.

In Exodus 34, we read that when Moses encountered the the presence of the Lord, it literally caused the skin of his face to shine with the glory of God. God's light physically transformed what it touched. When the children of Israel saw God's glory on Moses's skin, they were so afraid of him that Moses put a veil over his face whenever he spoke to them. Hidden under the veil, the Israelites couldn't see that, over time, the glory of Moses' face would begin to fade. But then, whenever Moses would return to have fellowship with the Lord, he removed the veil and again drank in God's glory.

Believe it or not, because we are covered by the righteousness of Jesus and have access to the baptism of the Holy Spirit, we actually have access to much more of God's glory than Moses did.

> Now if the ministry of death, chiseled in letters on stones, came with glory, so that the Israelites were not able to look directly at Moses' face because of the glory from his face — a fading glory — how will the ministry of the Spirit not be more glorious? For if the ministry of condemnation had glory, the ministry of righteousness overflows with even more glory. In fact, what had been glorious is not glorious now by comparison because of the glory that surpasses it. For if what was fading away was glorious, what endures will be even more glorious.
>
> Therefore, having such a hope, we use great boldness. **We are not like Moses, who used to put a veil over his face so that the Israelites could not stare at the end of what was fading away, but their minds were closed.** For to this day, at the reading of the old covenant, the same veil remains; it is not lifted, because it is set aside only in Christ. Even to this day, whenever Moses is read, a veil lies over their hearts, but whenever a person turns to the Lord, the veil is removed. Now the Lord is the Spirit, and where the Spirit of the Lord is, there is freedom. We all, with unveiled faces, are looking as in a mirror at the glory of the Lord and are being transformed into the same image from glory to glory; this is from the Lord who is the Spirit.
> 2 Corinthians 3:7-18 (HCSB)

As we walk in the Light of the Holy Spirit, we are being

transformed from mere reflectors into carriers of His glory. We have an invitation to take off the masks and behold a light that doesn't fade. We have the commission to leave our masks and old identities behind and shine Heaven's perfect light onto the world around us.

> Ascribe to Yahweh, you heavenly beings,
> ascribe to the Lord glory and strength.
> Ascribe to Yahweh the glory due His name;
> worship Yahweh
> in the splendor of His holiness.
> Psalm 29:1-2 (HCSB)

Through Christ Jesus, we have joined the angels as citizens of another kingdom. Every time we worship, we are answering an invitation to step into the beauty of God's holiness. So go and exalt Him with the glory He deserves. Go and drink in His perfect light that casts no shadow! Then go and make disciples!

> "In the same way, let your light shine before men, so that they may see your good works and give glory to your Father in heaven."
> Matthew 5:16 (HCSB).

Because we have freely received this gift from God, we owe the world a clear view of the bright light of Jesus. Do not hide from others what God has done in your life, but shout the testimony of Jesus with every breath in your lungs! Worship the Lord with every thought, word, and deed. May God ignite the sacrifice of your life so that you become a bright beacon of His glory to a world in darkness. May you become a cultural ambassador of Heaven here on the earth. May your life of worship be an altar upon which the glory of the Lord is enthroned and a monument of grace for all of creation to behold.

ABOUT THE AUTHOR

Wes Pickering is a passionate disciple of Jesus Christ. He is a husband to his wife Hannah. They live with their border collie Heidi in a little house with a yellow door in Nashville, Tennessee. Together, they are worship leaders who earnestly desire for people to encounter and be transformed by the presence of God. As a songwriter and musician, Wes had written and produced numerous albums and hundreds of songs. Wes speaks and leads worship year round at churches and events around the world. He and his wife Hannah are passionate about missions work and have taken up the call to bring God's glorious message of salvation to the ends of the earth. They are revivalists who long to see the will and kingdom of God come on earth as it is in heaven.

For more information, visit wespickering.com

www.ingramcontent.com/pod-product-compliance
Lightning Source LLC
Chambersburg PA
CBHW051944290426
44110CB00015B/2097